Janelle Ho and
Helen Pearson

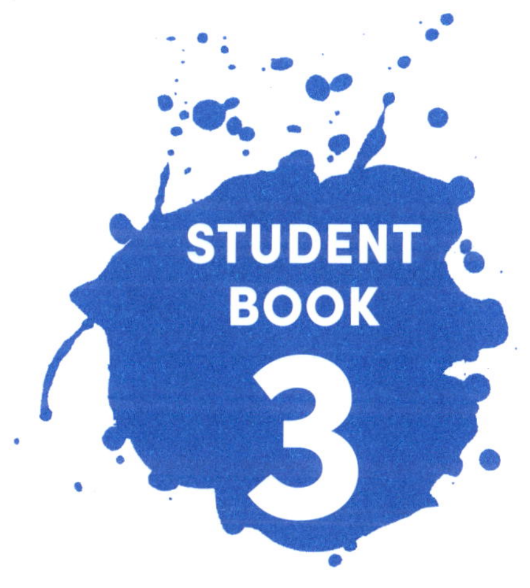

NSW Edition

Name: ______________________________

Class: ______________________________

CONTENTS

SLLURP

SLLURP summarises the spelling strategies that you can use to learn new words.

Say	Say the word carefully and slowly to yourself.
Listen	Listen to how each part of the word sounds in sequence.
Look	Look at the patterns of letters in the word and the shape of the word.
Understand	Understand rules, word meanings and word origins.
Remember	Remember all the similar words you can already spell and relate this knowledge to any new word.
Practise	Practise writing the word until it is firmly fixed in your long-term memory.

Spelling Rules! Student Book 3 (ISBN 9780655092605) © Janelle Ho, Helen Pearson

Scope and Sequence

Unit	SKILL FOCUS						WORD LIST
	Vowels	Consonants	Letter patterns	Morphology and etymology	Homophones/ Confusing words	Topic words	
1	a-e, i-e			-ed; irregular verbs and plurals	brake/break		brave, shade, brake, table, awake, aeroplane, while, beside, spite, alive, advise, promise
2	o-e, u-e			-ing, -y			close, alone, erode, suppose, approve, wardrobe, huge, pure, cube, refuse, accuse, conclude
3	oo, ee, ea, ai, oa				to/too/two, rowed/road/rode, great/grate		shook, blood, choose, soothe, bleed, breath, breathe, threat, explain, throat, poach, cockroach
4			ow, ou, oy ey, ay				know, growl, below, allow, touch, grouchy, pounce, mountain, royal, money, trolley, layer
5		ch, tch			cord/chord		arch, coach, attach, clench, monarch, technology, chemical, scheme, parachute, sketch, scratch, butcher
6	REVISION						
7	ie, ei				peace/piece, cheap/cheep, steel/steal		grief, relief, fierce, niece, sieve, thieve, believe, friend, weird, receive, ceiling, foreign
8	au, aw						taut, haul, fault, pause, sauce, sausage, audio, flaw, thaw, drawer, sprawl, awesome
9		medial double consonants					gallop, collide, swallow, channel, tennis, rubbish, common, lesson, borrow, attempt, affect, effect
10		silent letters: kn, wr	le				saddle, waddle, struggle, scribble, settle, drizzle, grumble, candle, stable, wobble, syllable, startle
11						months of the year	January, February, March, April, May, June, July, August, September, October, November, December
12	REVISION						
13		soft and hard g			great/grate, grown/groan, guest/guessed		gather, guest, guide, together, germ, gentle, genius, giant, large, stage, gigantic, gypsy
14			qu		quit/quiet/quite		quiet, quite, queue, quarter, squirm, squeal, squawk, equal, request, require, squirrel, mosquito
15			igh, eigh, aigh, ough, augh	irregular past tense verbs			delight, midnight, frighten, frightful, neighbour, height, straight, enough, though, through, daughter, naughty
16		gh, ph		tele, phone, photo, auto, graph			laugh, toughen, graph, photograph, autograph, elephant, telephone, sphere, trophy, alphabet, phrase, physical
17		words ending in f, ff, fe, ffe		changing f to v; collective nouns			puff, cliff, staff, shelf, wolf, scarf, wharf, thief, knife, handkerchief, yourself, giraffe
18	REVISION						
19		silent letters: kn, wr, t, gn, h, s, b				non-English words	wrinkle, wrestle, knead, knowledge, gnaw, gnome, hour, honest, island, tongue, doubt, ghost
20				words beginning with a-, al-			across, always, about, around, almost, already, ahead, asleep, above, another, along, altogether
21				un-, mis-, dis-			untidy, unlikely, mischief, misplace, misbehave, mistake, disagree, disgrace, disgusting, dishonest, disobey, discover
22				proper nouns, astrophes of possession		Australian states and territories, and capitals	country, state, northern, western, south, capital, territory, Australia, New South Wales, Victoria, Tasmania, Queensland
23				-er, -est		Aboriginal Australian words	Mob, Elder, Auntie, Uncle, deadly, gammon, tucker, humpy, yakka, yidaki, boomerang, marngrook
24	REVISION						
25				-ful, -less: changing y to i			harmful, peaceful, colourful, grateful, boastful, plentiful, beautiful, helpless, useless, careless, fearless, lifeless
26				-ness, -ion, -ship, -dom, -hood, -wards			kindness, happiness, revision, television, direction, friendship, kingdom, freedom, forwards, backwards, childhood, neighbourhood
27				uni-, bi-, tri-, kilo-, dec-, centi-, milli-		measurement	metre, kilometre, centimetre, millimetre, litre, gram, decade, uniform, bicycle, triangle, dozen, dollar
28			ex	in-			exit, extra, expert, experience, extreme, example, exact, excuse, excellent, exclaim, excite, exercise
29	words ending in o, oe, oo, a			irregular plurals	confusing words: there/their/they're		hero, piano, echo, radio, toe, canoe, kangaroo, taboo, sofa, drama, idea, era
30	REVISION						
31			ion	-ion			station, fiction, section, fraction, cushion, fashion, mission, expression, religion, million, champion, information
32				-ment			movement, statement, argument, amazement, measurement, government, environment, treatment, development, attachment, encouragement, disappointment
33				-able, -ible, -ly			reliable, capable, adorable, available, comfortable, miserable, valuable, horrible, terrible, sensible, flexible, responsible
34					desert/dessert, course/coarse	non-English words	igloo, robot, yacht, iceberg, khaki, tsunami, kindergarten, kowtow, pizza, spaghetti, chocolate, restaurant
35	REVISION						

NOTE TO TEACHERS AND PARENTS

Spelling Rules!

Some students are natural spellers, but the vast majority of students need formal, systematic and sequential instruction about the way spelling works and the strategies they can use to become independent, confident spellers.

The *Spelling Rules!* program is based on sound linguistic and pedagogical theory. It is informed by research into how students of different ages acquire and apply spelling skills, and how those skills move from the working to the long-term memory. The program closely follows the NSW English Syllabus. NSW Syllabus references are provided in the two Teacher Resource Books. The program consists of seven Student Books.

Each student book contains units of work, with each unit designed to be used over the course of a week. The content of each unit follows the suggested instructional sequence in the NSW English Syllabus. Each unit simultaneously develops new skills and reinforces skills from previous units. Where appropriate, topic words from other syllabus areas are included. When spelling rules and tips are introduced, only known sounds and letter patterns are used so that students focus on one skill at a time. Regular revision units enable teachers to assess student progress and reinforce key rules and patterns from previous units. Books 1 to 4 also include a simple reflection activity that encourages students to assess their own progress and provides you with a starting point for discussion.

Spelling knowledge

Learning to spell involves developing different kinds of spelling knowledge:

- **Kinaesthetic knowledge** – the physical feeling when saying different sounds and words, and when writing the shapes of letters and words
- **Phonological knowledge** – how a word sounds and the patterns of sounds in words
- **Visual knowledge** – how letters and words look and the visual patterns in words
- **Morphemic knowledge** – the meaning or function of words or parts of words
- **Etymological knowledge** – the origins and history of words and the effect this has on spelling patterns.

Icons used in Student Book 3

The following icons identify the main spelling strategy that students will use to complete an activity.

Say the word. (Kinaesthetic knowledge) These activities ask students to experience how sounds feel in the mouth and jaw. Changing the positions of the jaw, lips and tongue changes the sounds we make. Encourage students to pronounce the sounds and words accurately. If they mispronounce a sound or word, they may misrepresent it in writing.

Listen to the word. (Phonological knowledge) These activities focus on discriminating between different sounds and breaking up words into syllables or individual sound segments (phonemes).

Look at the word. (Visual knowledge) These activities help students to see how the sound is represented using combinations of letters, and to associate this visual pattern with what they are hearing. Students will develop the ability to know when a word does or does not 'look right'.

Understand the word. (Morphemic and etymological knowledge) These activities focus on word meanings, word families, prefixes and suffixes, spelling rules, word origins and so on, which help embed spelling in the long-term memory.

Practise writing the word. (Kinaesthetic knowledge) These activities develop students' awareness of the physical movement involved in writing the word. By practising writing the word a number of times and in different contexts, the spelling becomes embedded in the long-term memory.

This icon highlights useful spelling rules.

This icon tells students that a special clue or hint is provided for an activity. It may be a spelling, grammar or punctuation convention, or a definition of a useful term.

The reflection encourages students to assess their progress across each unit.

Student Book 3

Units of work

Student Book 3 contains 35 weekly units of work. See the **Scope and Sequence chart** on page 3 for more information. Each revision unit gives students an opportunity to self-assess.

Word lists

In *Student Book 3*, each unit (except Revision) has a list of spelling words. The core words in the lists have been chosen to support the learning focus and strategies being taught in the unit.

Spelling lists enable a spelling element to be focused on, and provide sufficient examples to consolidate the teaching point. Topic words come from other curriculum areas, such as mathematics and social sciences. In addition, homophones and words that are easily confused with each other are explained and practised.

SLLURP

Each word list begins with a reminder for students to SLLURP. SLLURP summarises the strategies that will help spelling move from students' working memory to their long-term memory. These strategies are provided on page 2, for easy reference.

Unit at a glance

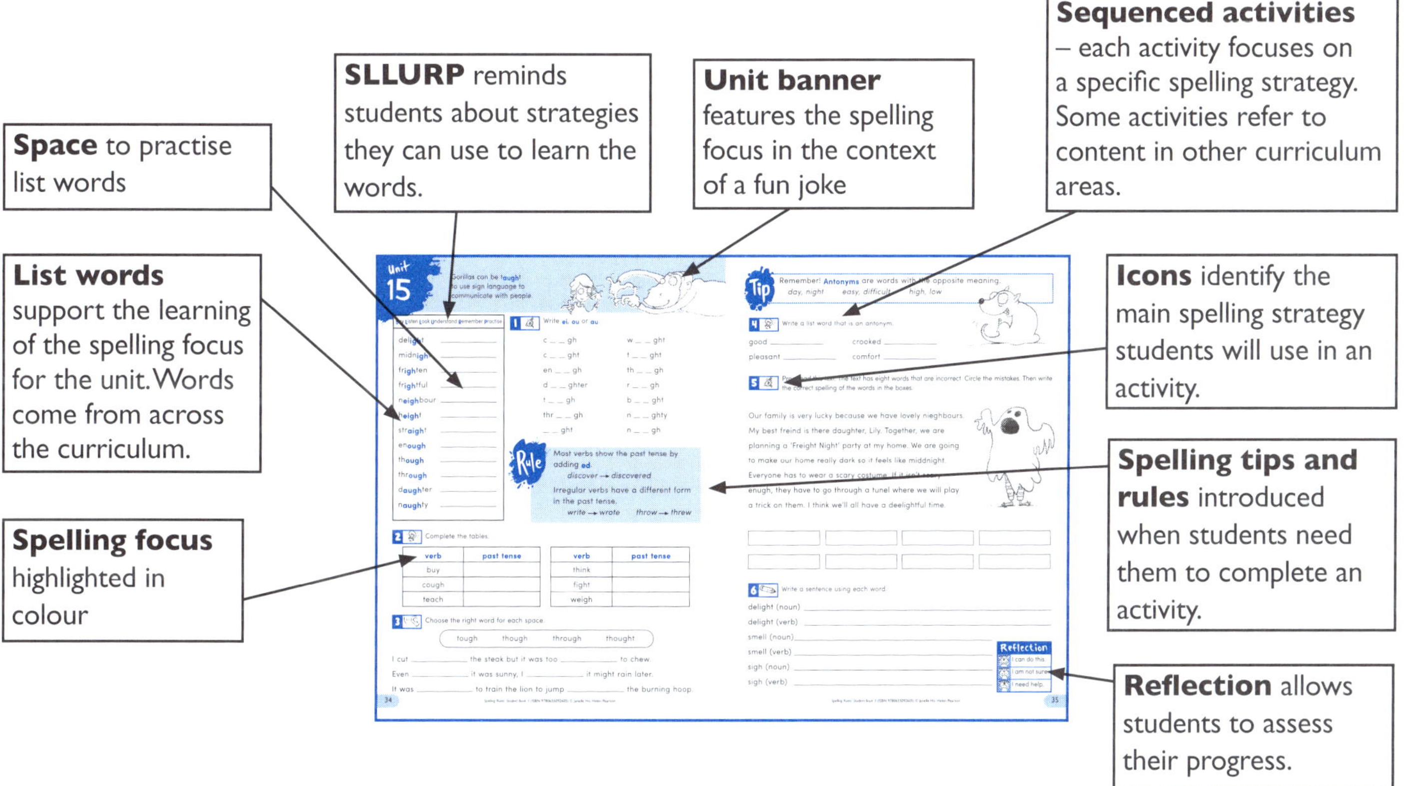

Spelling Rules! Teacher Resource Book 3–6

Full teacher support for *Student Book 3* is provided by *Spelling Rules! Teacher Resource Book 3–6*. Here you will find valuable background information about spelling development and spelling knowledge, along with practical resources, such as:

- teaching tips for every unit in *Student Book 3*
- extra word lists
- strategies for teaching spelling
- guidelines for assessment and diagnosis of errors
- activities to support struggling spellers
- worthwhile extension for more able spellers.

Unit 1

Tapeworms can live inside people. They can be up to 25 metres long – that's the length of two buses!

Say Listen Look Understand Remember Practise

brave	________
shade	________
brake	________
table	________
awake	________
aeroplane	________
while	________
beside	________
spite	________
alive	________
advise	________
promise	________

1 Find a list word that rhymes. Write another word that follows the **a-e** or **i-e** pattern.

gain	________	________
lied	________	________
label	________	________
smile	________	________
drive	________	________
quite	________	________
save	________	________
stayed	________	________

Write the two list words that have the same ending but do not rhyme.

________ ________

2 Write an **a-e** word to match each meaning.

f_ _ _	the front of your head
sh_ _ _	you don't do this if you want a beard
sn_ _ _	a reptile with no legs
br_ _ _	willing to face danger

3 Write an **i-e** word to match each meaning.

sl_ _ _	slip downwards
pr_ _ _	what something costs
m_ _ _	more than one mouse
in_ _ _ _	not outside

Spelling Rules! Student Book 3 (ISBN 9780655092605) © Janelle Ho, Helen Pearson

4 Colour the correct word.

Boil the eggs in a | pan | pane | of water, then cool them in a | tub | tube |.

Our | car | care | was parked for too long and we got a | fin | fine |.

Tomatoes turn red when they are | rip | ripe |.

Rule For most verbs ending in **e**, you drop the **e** before adding **ed** to make the past tense. *live* → *lived* *bake* → *baked*

But be careful: some verbs do not follow this rule!

make → *made* *drive* → *drove* *wake* → *woke*

5 Complete each sentence by writing the verb in the past tense.

Jane ____________ (blame) her dog for messing up her homework.

Mrs Smith ____________ (advise) us to read for 20 minutes each day.

Sanjay ____________ (slide) on the wet leaves and hurt his foot.

Mum ____________ (leave) a message for Dad. I ____________ (write) it down but I think I've ____________ (lose) the piece of paper.

Rule Most nouns ending in **e** make the plural by adding **s** but some do not.

house → *houses* but *mouse* → *mice*

6 Write the plural for each noun.

table ____________ goose ____________ aeroplane ____________

fire ____________ crime ____________ man ____________

7 The words **break** and **brake** are homophones. Write the correct homophone.

Don't ____________ too quickly or you'll fall off the bike.

Don't ____________ your stride while you run.

Reflection

I can do this.

I am not sure.

I need help.

Unit 2

The funny bone is not actually a bone. It is a nerve behind your elbow.

Say Listen Look Understand Remember Practise

close	______
alone	______
erode	______
suppose	______
approve	______
wardrobe	______
huge	______
pure	______
cube	______
refuse	______
accuse	______
conclude	______

1

Words can rhyme but be spelt differently. Find a list word that rhymes.

knows	toes	______
load	glowed	______
moan	blown	______
brood	glued	______
	stews	______
	groove	______

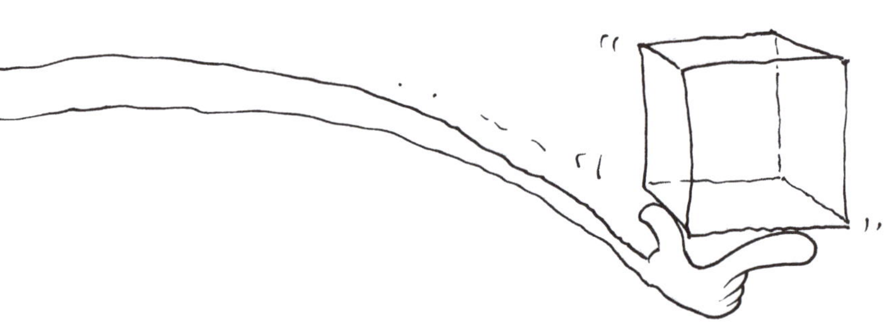

2

Use the clues to write **o-e** and **u-e** words. The mystery word is a shape.

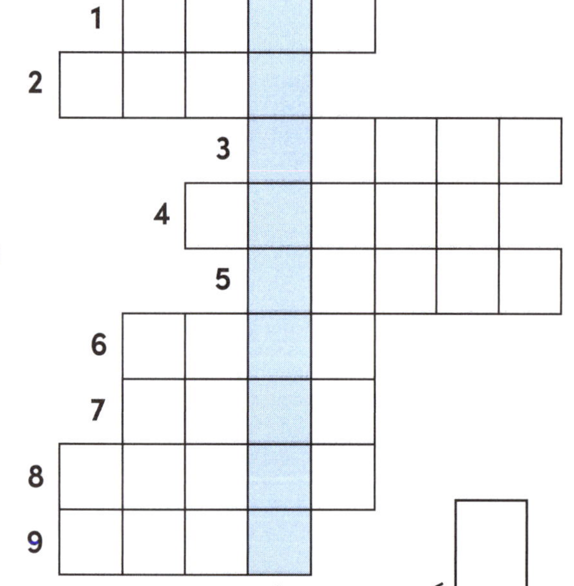

1. not spoilt or dirty
2. I _ _ _ _ _ you!
3. Please _ _ _ _ _ _ the door.
4. a piece of rock
5. all by yourself
6. Have you _ _ _ _ _ your work?
7. very large
8. complete
9. an object with six square sides

Mystery word: ______________

Spelling Rules! Student Book 3 (ISBN 9780655092605) © Janelle Ho, Helen Pearson

3 There are many ways to say *big*. Arrange these words in alphabetical order.

huge large gigantic enormous great

____

4 Syllables are the beats in a word. Write how many syllables you hear in each shape word.

prism  cylinder  cube  sphere 

For words that end in **e**, drop the **e** to add **ing**.

love → *loving* *use* → *using*

Drop the **e** to add **y** to make the adjective. *ice* → *icy*

5 Add **ing**.

close ____________ approve ____________ amaze ____________

refuse ____________ conclude ____________ promise ____________

6 Write the adjective by adding **y**.

not liking work (laze) ____________ bright, glowing (shine) ____________

having many bones, thin (bone) ____________

hard to please (choose) ____________

7 Each set of words has the same spelling pattern, but one word sounds different. Circle the word with a different sound and then use it in your own sentence.

sure pure cure	______________________________

dove love move	______________________________

Reflection

- I can do this.
- I am not sure.
- I need help.

Unit 3

It is easier to float in sea water than in fresh water.

Say Listen Look Understand Remember Practise	
shook	______
blood	______
choose	______
soothe	______
bleed	______
breath	______
breathe	______
threat	______
explain	______
throat	______
poach	______
cockroach	______

1 Rearrange the letters to make a list word.

ooksh	ldobo	cpoha
______	______	______
soecho	rteath	theebar
______	______	______
bedel	laxinep	thorta
______	______	______

2 Add another word to make a compound word.

door______ tooth______

moon______ ______spoon

broom______ ______room

3 Write the word in the plural.

breath ______ street ______ tooth ______

year ______ goose ______ cockroach ______

4 Add the correct suffix to these verbs. Choose from **s**, **ed** or **ing**.

Dad is sweep____ the leaves from the driveway.

The wind blew my hat into the water. Luckily, it float____.

I hope we see a rainbow when the sun break____ through the clouds.

After our bushwalk, we feast____ on hot damper with honey.

Auntie Jean poach____ an egg for breakfast this morning.

Spelling Rules! Student Book 3 (ISBN 9780655092605) © Janelle Ho, Helen Pearson

5 These pairs of words are related: **blood–bleed**, **breath–breathe**. Which are nouns and which are verbs?

noun ______________ ______________

verb ______________ ______________

6 Write one from the pairs: **blood–bleed**, **breath–breathe**.

Be careful! If you cut yourself, you will ______________.

I think there is a lot of ______________ but Mum says it's only a tiny cut.

______________ deeply so you won't feel so out of ______________.

7 Add **e** to the noun to make the verb. Circle the parts of the word that change when you say the new word.

breath ______________ bath ______________

cloth ______________ teeth ______________

8 Colour the correct homophone.

I need | to | too | two | eggs | to | too | two | make a cake.

Cheng Mai is | to | too | two | sick to come | to | too | two | the party.

May I watch television | to | too | two |?

Foong | rowed | road | rode | ten kilometres on his bike.

Please | grate | great | the carrots.

9 Add a letter to make a new word. Use the clue! Colour the circle if the vowel sound changes.

○ heat → ______________ (grain used to make flour)

○ beat → ______________ (wild animal)

○ read → ______________ (...! Steady! Go!)

○ treat → ______________ (warning meant to frighten)

Reflection

I can do this.

I am not sure.

I need help.

Unit 4

Bamboo can grow up to 91 centimetres in one day.

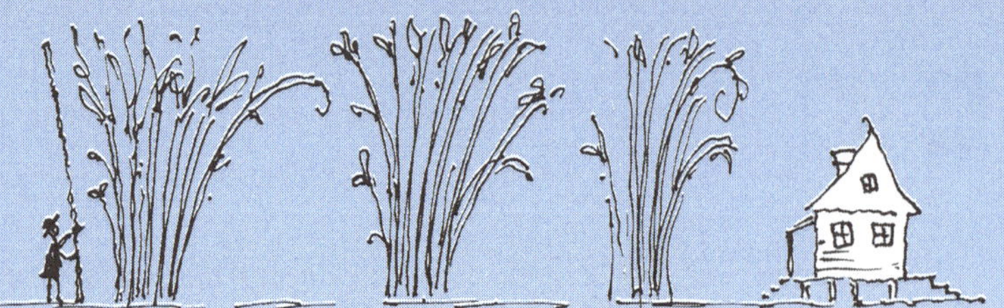

Say Listen Look Understand Remember Practise

know	______
growl	______
below	______
allow	______
touch	______
grouchy	______
pounce	______
mountain	______
royal	______
money	______
trolley	______
layer	______

1 Write each verb in the past tense.

verb	past tense
know	
blow	
draw	
chew	
allow	

2 Write list words in the correct category.

adjective	both a noun and a verb
______	______
______	______
	______

3 Make a new word by changing the first letter in each list word. The clues give the meaning of the new word.

list word	new word	clue
mountain	______	water spouting
money	______	what bees make
royal	______	faithful
touch	______	where a joey sleeps
growl	______	move when hunting

4 Fill in the missing letters to name three animals.

d _ _ key   m _ _ k _ _   t _ _ k _ _

Spelling Rules! Student Book 3 (ISBN 9780655092605) © Janelle Ho, Helen Pearson

5 Fill in the missing letters to make rhyming words. Add your own words.

_ _ower  _ _ower  _ower  ____________

_ _own  _ _own  _ _own  ____________

6 Proofread this diary entry. There are five words that are incorrect. Circle the mistakes. Then write the correct spelling of the words in the boxes.

Today Mum and I found a strey dog. The tag on his collar said he was called Honey. I made a poster and stuck it on our fence. I tied a rope to Honey's collar and we walked around the block. At first he was growchy. Then he tried to run a way. Mum's phone rang. It was Honey's owner. When she collected him, she offered me some mony but I refused. We all enjoyd seeing Honey jump up to proudly walk off with his owner.

7 Unjumble these letters. The words are all days of the week. Remember to use a capital letter.

difray ____________ dratyusa ____________

saddenwey ____________ trayshud ____________

manyod ____________ yestuda ____________

Which day haven't you used? ____________

8 Say each word. Circle one word with a different vowel sound.

south	grouch	proud
found	pout	mouth
touch	ounce	blouse

Unit 5

In 1802, André-Jacques Garnerin jumped from a height of 2400 metres using a parachute.

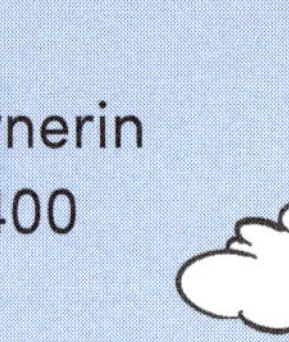

Say Listen Look Understand Remember Practise	
arch	______
coach	______
attach	______
clench	______
monarch	______
technology	______
chemical	______
scheme	______
parachute	______
sketch	______
scratch	______
butcher	______

Tip

ch can begin or end a word.
tch can never begin a word.

1 Say each word. What sound does **ch** make? Use colours to separate them into two groups.

coach	teacher	school
choose	scheme	clench
pinch	much	monarch
ache	chemical	challenge

2 Say each word. What sound does **tch** make? Write a **ch** list word that makes the same sound.

fetch	catch	itchy
kitchen	butcher	watch

ch word: ______

3 Write **ch** or **tch**.

____ oice	wi ____	whi ____
____ oir	stoma ____	____ erry
bu ____ er	stre ____	____ aracter
an ____ or	ki ____ en	a ____ ieve

4 Say each word. Answer the questions with complete sentences.

chef	machine	charade	chauffeur

What sound does **ch** make?

______

Which list word has the same sound?

______

Spelling Rules! Student Book 3 (ISBN 9780655092605) © Janelle Ho, Helen Pearson

If a word ends in a **ch** sound, add **es**.
If a word ends in a **k** sound, add **s**.

5 Add **s** or **es** to make the plural.

one arch, two ______________

one coach, two ______________

one monarch, two ______________

one sketch, two ______________

one crutch, two ______________

one stomach, two ______________

6 Write the plural.

Singular	Plural
chemical	
butcher	
scheme	

Singular	Plural
technology	
cockroach	
duchess	

Tip

cord and **chord** are homophones.
cord = wire or a strong string
chord = three or more musical notes played together

7 Write the correct word.

Tie up the ____________ or someone could trip over it.

After I learn to play notes on the piano, I will learn to play ____________ .

8 There is a mistake in every sentence. Circle it and write the correct word.

Jill attatched the cord from the trailer to the bike.

____

The pain from the injection made me klench my fist.

____

Not all chemicles are bad but some are toxic indeed.

____

One of my favurite acts in the parade is the parachute jump.

____

Some **lee**ches can suck out ten times their own weight in human blood.

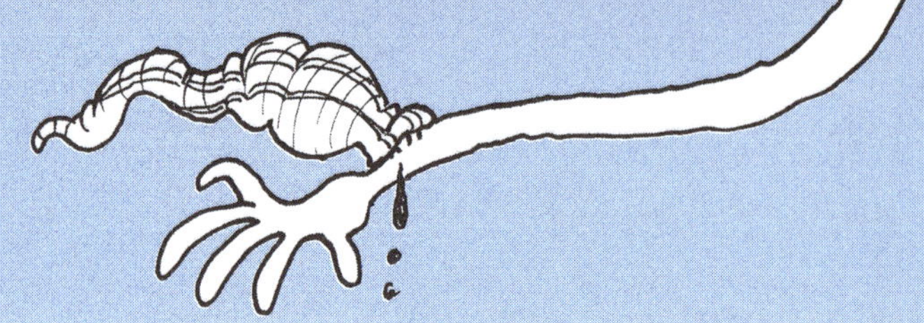

1 Add a letter to make a new word.

too ____________ lose ____________ sleep ____________

pant ____________ lie ____________ cord ____________

2 Colour the correct word.

My pyjamas have red and white | strips | stripes |.

We wrote the shopping list on a | scrap | scrape | of paper.

Do you like playing | hid | hide | and seek?

'Put your homework in the | tub | tube | on my desk,' said the teacher.

3 Write the correct homophone.

to too two	Omar drew a person with __________ eyes but three noses! Kelly loves going __________ the movies when it is raining. Bill has red hair. His twin sister does __________ .

brake break	If you ____________ anything, you'll have to pay for it. Remember to ____________ as you near the corner.

4 Colour the correct form of the verb.

I | hope | hoped | the test wouldn't be hard, but it was!

Sam | did | done | his homework before playing hockey.

Kelly | loves | loved | going to the movies when it is raining.

It was Mum's birthday, so I | make | made | her a cake.

Everyone | know | knew | about the party except Dad.

Spelling Rules! Student Book 3 (ISBN 9780655092605) © Janelle Ho, Helen Pearson

5 Write **ee** or **ea** to complete these words.

p _ _ ch   str _ _ t   scr _ _ m   cl _ _ n   sl _ _ p

tr _ _   dr _ _ m   j _ _ ns   fr _ _   _ _ t

6 Write **oa** or **ow** to complete these words.

gr _ _   fl _ _ ted   bel _ _   sh _ _ ed   l _ _ d

kn _ _   pill _ _   f _ _ m   wind _ _   sl _ _

7 Write **ou** or **ow** to complete these words.

sh _ _ t   cl _ _ n   fr _ _ n   c _ _ nt   f _ _ nd

br _ _ n   pr _ _ d   r _ _ nd   dr _ _ ned   cr _ _ n

8 Write **ch** or **tch** to complete these words.

_____ oose   rea _____   ki _____ en   _____ eer   ar _____

s _____ eme   scra _____   atta _____   fe _____   te _____ nology

9 Write a list word.

Group	**Example**
shape	square, triangle, rectangle, ____________
furniture	chair, desk, ____________, ____________
transport	train, car, ____________
____________	king, queen, empress, emperor
insect	fly, bug, caterpillar, ____________
hand actions	clap, wave, sign, ____________, ____________

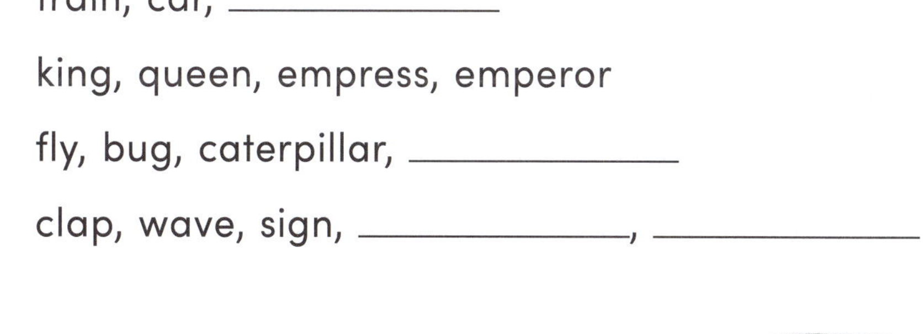

Unit 7

People used to believe the Earth was flat, and that if you walked far enough, you'd fall off!

Say Listen Look Understand Remember Practise

grief ______
relief ______
fierce ______
niece ______
sieve ______
thieve ______
believe ______
friend ______
weird ______
receive ______
ceiling ______
foreign ______

1 Find a list word that rhymes.

leaf ______ peeling ______ crease ______

leave ______ mend ______ beard ______

2 Write a list word for each clue.

not native ______

the daughter of your brother or sister ______

a container with holes ______

sadness ______

steal ______

accept ______

3 Make another **ie** word by changing one letter.

pierce ______ relieve ______ grief ______ niece ______

4 Follow the example to complete the table.

noun	verb	sentence (using either word)
grief	grieve	My neighbour cried with grief when his dog died.
	relieve	
belief		
thief		

Spelling Rules! Student Book 3 (ISBN 9780655092605) © Janelle Ho, Helen Pearson

Use the clues to complete the words. Colour the word with **ie**.

Clue					
a caterpillar's favourite food			E		F
the top of a house		R			F
the person in charge			I		F
meat from a cow				E	F
not able to hear		D			F
bread is baked in this shape		L			F
1 ÷ 2 =				L	F
a game played with a club		G			F
a flat surface to put things on			E		F
a dangerous hunting animal		W			F

Learn these homophones:

piece = a part
peace = not at war
cheap = not expensive
cheep = sound of a bird
steel = type of metal
steal = thieve or rob

Colour the correct word.

Jack tried to | steel | steal | a | piece | peace | of cake.

Everyone wants to live in | piece | peace |.

The chicks | cheap | cheep | noisily when they are hungry.

Movie tickets are | cheap | cheep | on Tuesdays.

Find a list word that belongs to each group.

steal	burgle	______________	mate	buddy	______________
cousin	nephew	______________	wall	floor	______________
odd	strange	______________	scary	wild	______________

Write one sentence using both words.

friend
piece

____

____

Unit 8

The first **sau**sage may have been made more than 5000 years ago! **Aw**esome!

Say **L**isten **L**ook **U**nderstand **R**emember **P**ractise

t**au**t	________
h**au**l	________
f**au**lt	________
p**au**se	________
s**au**ce	________
s**au**sage	________
audio	________
fl**aw**	________
th**aw**	________
dr**aw**er	________
spr**aw**l	________
awesome	________

1 Write **au** or **aw**.

l _ _	dr _ _	bec _ _ se
t _ _ t	s _ _ ce	_ _ ful
y _ _ n	_ _ dio	h _ _ l
p _ _ se	th _ _	r _ _

2 Write a list word.

________ ________ ________

3 Add a suffix to make a word family. Not all suffixes will be used.

Base word	add **s**	add **ed**	add **ing**
haul			
fault			
pause			
sausage		X	X
flaw			X
thaw			
drawer		X	X
sprawl			

Spelling Rules! Student Book 3 (ISBN 9780655092698) © Janelle Ho, Helen Pearson

4 Write a list word that rhymes.

salt	crawl	shores	door	four
______	______	______	______	______

All the words have the same vowel sound. Write all the ways to make this sound.

____

5 Unscramble the letters to make a list word.

wraedr	iodua	pwarls	oasweem	gaseusa
______	______	______	______	______

6 Choose the correct homophone.

The smell of [raw | roar] [meat | meet] makes the hungry animals [raw | roar].

Mr Paul's shoulder is still [saw | sore]. He hurt the muscle when he tried out his [new | knew] [saw | sore].

Oh no! Did Shaun [draw | drawer] all over the [blew | blue] [draws | drawers]? No. He [threw | through] finger paint on the [flaw | floor].

[Paw | Poor | Pour] some milk into the dish for the [paw | poor | pour] cat.

7 Synonyms are words with the same meaning. Antonyms are words with opposite meanings. Write a list word.

synonym	list word	antonym
tight	______	loose
melt	______	freeze
rest	______	continue
amazing	______	boring
______	______	virtue

Reflection

- I can do this.
- I am not sure.
- I need help.

Unit 9

When a horse gallops, all four hooves are off the ground at once.

Say Listen Look Understand Remember Practise	
gallop	______
collide	______
swallow	______
channel	______
tennis	______
rubbish	______
common	______
lesson	______
borrow	______
attempt	______
affect	______
effect	______

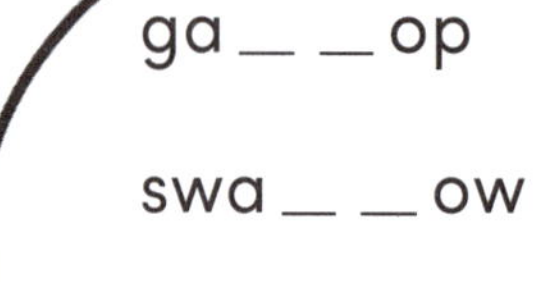

1 The words in each balloon are missing the same double letters. Write the missing letters.

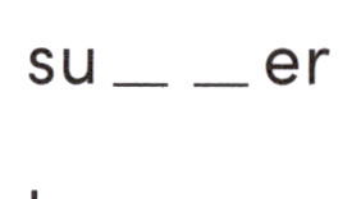

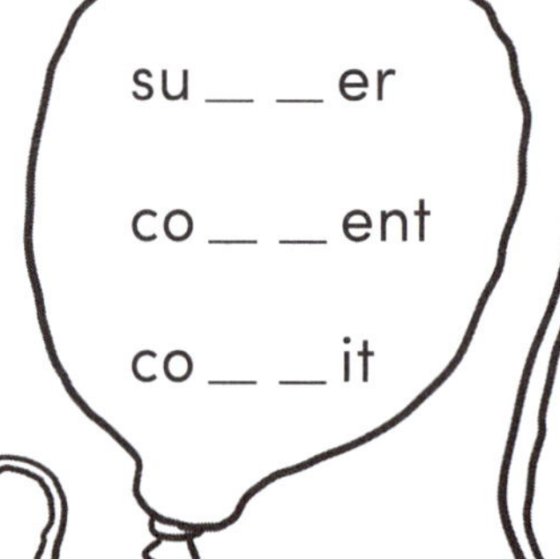

ga _ _ op
swa _ _ ow
va _ _ ey

su _ _ er
ha _ _ en
su _ _ ose

su _ _ er
co _ _ ent
co _ _ it

su _ _ en
gi _ _ y
ri _ _ le

2 Use the clue to complete each word.

_ ff _ _ _	cause a change
_ _ rr _ _	a long orange vegetable
_ _ rr _ _	what you do with books in a library
_ _ nn _ _	a racket game played with a yellow ball
_ _ mm _ _	a tool for hitting nails
_ _ mm _ _	shared by everyone
_ _ dd _ _	useful for reaching high places
_ _ ll _ _ _	crash together
_ _ bb _ _ _	litter
_ tt _ _ _ _	try

Spelling Rules! Student Book 3 (ISBN 9780655092605) © Janelle Ho, Helen Pearson

The words **affect** and **effect** are often confused.
affect (verb) = cause a change
effect (noun) = result of a change

3 Write the correct word. You may need to add a suffix.

The assembly talk had a positive ______________ on the students.

The noise is ______________ Billy's ability to focus.

For our science project, we learned how light ______________ plants.

One ______________ is that plants grow towards light.

4 Choose one word from each box to make compound words.

letter	wheel	grass	button	pillow	bitter
hopper	box	hole	sweet	barrow	case

______________ ______________ ______________

______________ ______________ ______________

5 Circle the words that need double letters and write them correctly.

We never leave rubish in our backyard. But last night my dog, Oscar, knocked over the bin and the lid came of. A posum colected some stale bread and buter and ate it for diner. Then it started to galop noisily over our roof. Dad used a lader to climb up and shoo it away. I tied Oscar in his kenel because he was trying to burow under the fence. He quickly slipped out of his colar and ran away. What a busy night!

______________ ______________

______________ ______________

______________ ______________

____

____

____

____

____

Reflection

- I can do this.
- I am not sure.
- I need help.

Unit 10

The first bubblegum was made in ancient Greece from tree resin.

Say Listen Look Understand Remember Practise	
saddle	________
waddle	________
struggle	________
scribble	________
settle	________
drizzle	________
grumble	________
candle	________
stable	________
wobble	________
syllable	________
startle	________

1 Make new words by adding **le** to these words.

buck ________ tack ________

pick ________ start ________

chuck ________ sing ________

trick ________ tang ________

tick ________ bang ________

crack ________ stab ________

2 Answer the following questions.

Which list word has more than two syllables?

____

Which three list words have long vowel sounds?

________ ________ ________

Tip The **schwa** (pronounced sh-wah) is a short vowel sound that is very common in English. It sounds like 'uh'.
The schwa is represented by many different letters.
tak**e**n s**u**ppose app**le** b**a**nan**a**

3 Say each word. Underline the letters that make the schwa.

pencil	brother	drizzle	parrot	bubble
about	lesson	channel	balloon	syllable

4 Fill in missing vowels so that these words are in alphabetical order.

scr__bble scr__mble scr__bble sc__ffle sc__ttle

Spelling Rules! Student Book 3 (ISBN 9780655092605) © Janelle Ho, Helen Pearson

The **k** in **kn** is a silent letter. *knuckle*
The **w** in **wr** is a silent letter. *wriggle*

Fill in the missing silent letter. Choose **k** or **w**.

_nee 

_nuckle 

_rite 

_rist 

_rong 

_not 

_nife

_nit

_riggle

Here are some interesting words to use instead of *talk*. Write the words in the correct speech bubble.

jabber	bellow	mutter	shout
whisper	gabble	roar	mumble
shriek	murmur	babble	chatter

talk loudly

______
______
______
______

talk quietly

______ ______
______ ______

talk quickly

______
______
______
______

Write a list word to complete these book titles and their authors.

Mrs ______ writes a note by Han Writing

What to do in a blackout by Light A. ______

It's only a ______! by Rain Coat

Animal Walk by Duck E. ______

Farm and ______ by Ina Country

My ______ about bear porridge by Goldilocks

Reflection

I can do this.
I am not sure.
I need help.

Unit 11

The Roman emperor Julius Caesar named the month of July after himself.

Say Listen Look Understand Remember Practise

January	___
February	___
March	___
April	___
May	___
June	___
July	___
August	___
September	___
October	___
November	___
December	___

1 Unjumble the letters for each month. Don't forget to start with a capital letter!

luyj	jurayan
___	___
bemveron	aym
___	___
tugusa	fryubare
___	___
recembed	charm
___	___
enju	brotoce
___	___
perbmeets	prail
___	___

2 How many days are there in each month? Use the number clues to complete this rhyme.

Clue: January = 1 December = 12

Thirty days have ___ (9), ___ (4), ___ (6)

and ___ (11).

All the rest have thirty-one,

Except for ___ (2) alone

Which has twenty-eight days clear

And twenty-nine in each leap year!

Calendar

Spelling Rules! Student Book 3 (ISBN 9780655092605) © Janelle Ho, Helen Pearson

 Write the months that match each season. Which is your favourite month? Why?

summer	autumn	winter	spring
________	________	________	________
________	________	________	________
________	________	________	________

My favourite month is ______________________________________

____

Proper nouns name people, places, pets, days of the week, months, books and poems. Proper nouns are always written with a capital letter.

 Circle the nouns that need capital letters in these sentences.

My uncle josh is driving his caravan from sydney to perth next july.

It was my birthday last friday and grandad gave me a book about mt everest.

easter sunday moves each year but is always in march or april.

 Write a sentence using as many proper nouns as you can that begin with the same letter.

Jillian Jones, who was born in January, lives on Jack Street in Jindabyne.

____

____

 Complete the table to build word families.

noun	adjective	compound word or noun group
	daily	daytime
week		
		lunar month
		leap year

Reflection
- I can do this.
- I am not sure.
- I need help.

Unit 12 Revision

There are more than 200 words for rain in the Hawaiian language. There are at least three different words for dri**zzle**.

 1 Make a new word by adding a consonant at the beginning. Can you add two?

_tale	_each	_our	_harp	_ear
_nail	_port	_lame	_lean	_are

 2 Make a new word by adding a letter at the end.

ski_	she_	rid_	was_	pea_
not_	dam_	grin_	bat_	win_

3 Make a new word by adding an extra vowel.

pin ______________	man ______________	shut ______________
bat ______________	flat ______________	rod ______________

Rule Two-syllable words with a double consonant break into syllables between the consonants.

puddle = pud/dle   *tennis = ten/nis*   *possum = pos/sum*

 4 Mark the syllable breaks in these words. In the circle, write the number of syllables you hear.

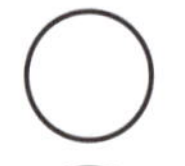

January ◯	April ◯	July ◯
giggle ◯	explain ◯	approve ◯
balloon ◯	rubbish ◯	relief ◯
startle ◯	technology ◯	audio ◯

Spelling Rules! Student Book 3 (ISBN 9780655092605) © Janelle Ho, Helen Pearson

5 All the words have a schwa. Write the letter(s) that represent the sound.

less _____ n   _____ wake   awes _____ me   for _____ gn   Aug _____ st

sett _____   wint _____   roy _____ l   mount _____ n   curr _____ nt

6 Add the suffix shown to each base word.

empty + ed ________________   juggle + ing ________________

butcher + s ________________   coach + ed ________________

believe + ing ________________   layer + s ________________

win + er ________________   sprawl + ing ________________

wobble + y ________________   breath + s ________________

7 Where does each animal live?

dog ______________   horse ______________   wombat ______________

rabbit ______________   bird ______________   pig ______________

goldfish ______________   bee ______________   owl ______________

sheep ______________   worm ______________

Tip An **anagram** is formed by rearranging the letters in a word. *Lemon* is an anagram of *melon*.

8 Arrange the letters to make an anagram.

wired ______________   warder ______________   steal ______________

sauce ______________   arches ______________   bleat ______________

9 Imagine you found a locked drawer. Write a story about what you found in there.

____

____

____

____

Unit 13

The big red spot on the planet Jupiter is a **gig**antic storm. It's three times the size of Earth, and hundreds of years old!

Say Listen Look Understand Remember Practise	
gather	____________
guest	____________
guide	____________
to**g**ether	____________
germ	____________
gentle	____________
genius	____________
giant	____________
lar**ge**	____________
sta**ge**	____________
gigantic	____________
gypsy	____________

1 Say each list word aloud and listen to the sound the **g** makes. Write the word inside the appropriate shape.

soft **g** as in gem

____
____
____
____
____
____
____

hard **g** as in gate

____
____
____
____

soft **g** and hard **g**

____

2 Look at the words in the gem and on the gate. Fill in the missing letters for the two rules.

g is usually soft when the next letter is _, _ or _.

g is usually hard when the next letter is _, _ or _.

3 Say these words aloud. Put a tick in the box if they follow the rules above. Put a cross in the box if they don't.

gather ☐	golf ☐	together ☐	generally ☐
giggle ☐	gaze ☐	guard ☐	gymnastics ☐

 4 Make a new word by adding a suffix from the box.

ly ed er th ful ing

grace______ guess______ grow______ great______

glad______ garden______ groan______ grin______

 5 Make an adjective by adding **y**. Remember your spelling rules.

noun	adjective
greed	
gloom	
guilt	
grease	
gas	

 6 Complete the table.

singular	plural
gypsy	
grocery	
guest	
genius	
gentleman	

7 Here are some interesting words you can use instead of *big* and *little*. Write the name of an animal that fits each adjective.

a gigantic ________________

a giant ________________

an enormous ________________

a huge ________________

a large ________________

a microscopic ________________

a miniscule ________________

a miniature ________________

a tiny ________________

 8 Colour the correct word.

Great | Grate the apple – not your finger!

You have grown | groan so tall this year.

Everyone guest | guessed who would win.

Reflection

I can do this.

I am not sure.

I need help.

Unit 14

The Atlantic giant **squ**id has the biggest eyes of any creature. One squid had eyes 50 centimetres in diameter.

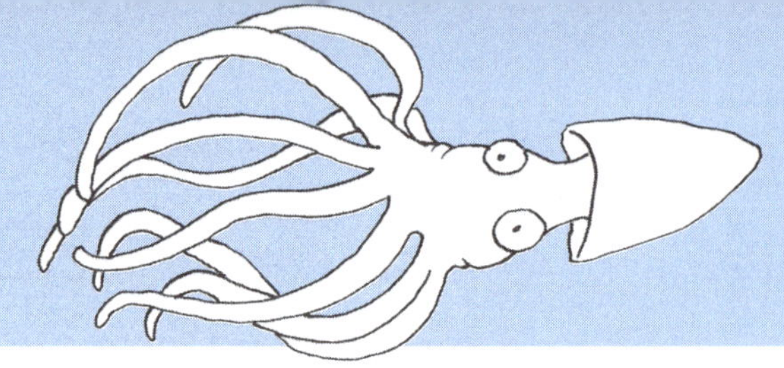

Say Listen Look Understand Remember Practise	
quiet	______
quite	______
queue	______
quarter	______
s**qu**irm	______
s**qu**eal	______
s**qu**awk	______
e**qu**al	______
re**qu**est	______
re**qu**ire	______
s**qu**irrel	______
mos**qu**ito	______

Rule

qu is always followed by another vowel.
cw and **qw** don't go together in English.

1

Fill in the missing vowels to make list words.

sq_ _r_   _q_ _l   q_ _ _t

q_ _t_   sq_ _ _l   q_ _rt_r

q_ _ _ _   r_q_ _st

2

Fill in the missing letters. Match the word to its meaning.

_qu_	a test
_ _qu_ _	one of a kind
_ _ _qu_	a jet of water
qu_ _ _ _ _ _	a colour
qu_ _	amount
_qu_ _ _	fluid

3

Use your dictionary to find these words starting with **squ**.

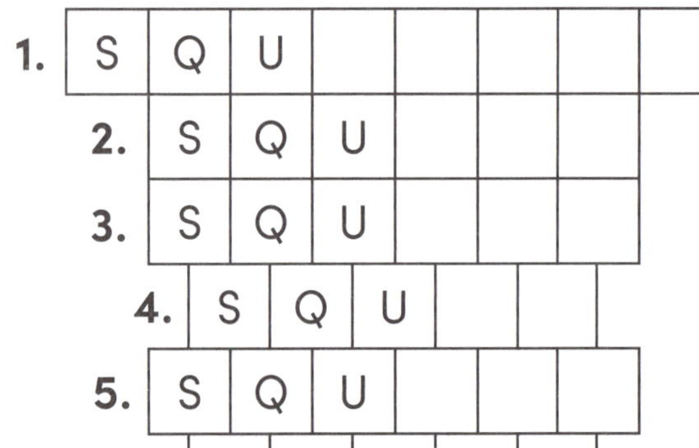

1. small furry animal
2. press together
3. look with eyes partly closed
4. sea animals with long tentacles
5. short high sound
6. crouch with a straight back
7. sound a parrot makes
8. shapes with four equal sides
9. line with twists or curves

Spelling Rules! Student Book 3 (ISBN 9780655092698) © Janelle Ho, Helen Pearson

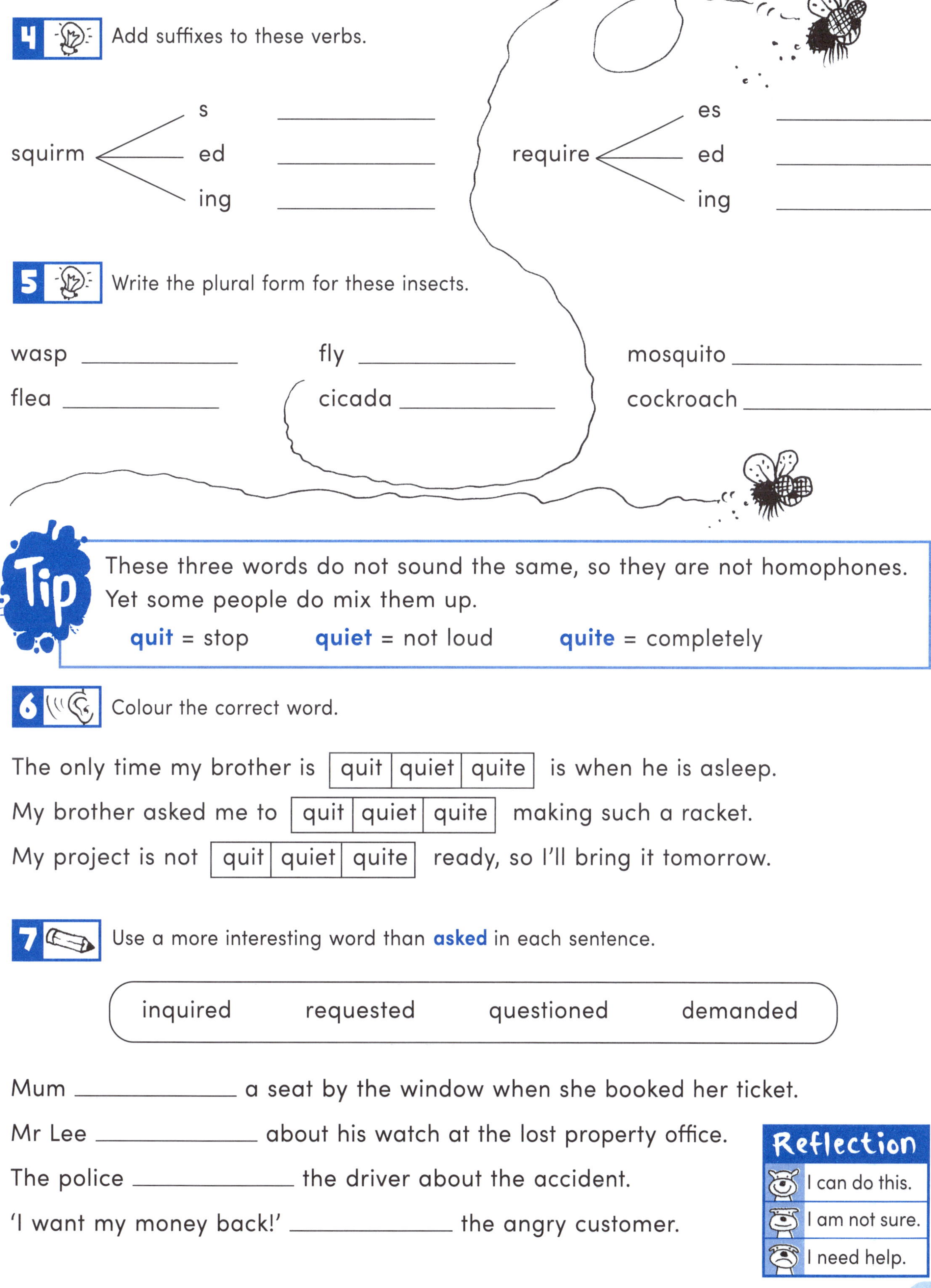

4 Add suffixes to these verbs.

squirm — s ____________ / ed ____________ / ing ____________

require — es ____________ / ed ____________ / ing ____________

5 Write the plural form for these insects.

wasp ____________ fly ____________ mosquito ____________

flea ____________ cicada ____________ cockroach ____________

Tip

These three words do not sound the same, so they are not homophones. Yet some people do mix them up.

quit = stop **quiet** = not loud **quite** = completely

6 Colour the correct word.

The only time my brother is | quit | quiet | quite | is when he is asleep.

My brother asked me to | quit | quiet | quite | making such a racket.

My project is not | quit | quiet | quite | ready, so I'll bring it tomorrow.

7 Use a more interesting word than **asked** in each sentence.

inquired requested questioned demanded

Mum ____________ a seat by the window when she booked her ticket.

Mr Lee ____________ about his watch at the lost property office.

The police ____________ the driver about the accident.

'I want my money back!' ____________ the angry customer.

Reflection

I can do this.

I am not sure.

I need help.

Unit 15

Gorillas can be **taught** to use sign language to communicate with people.

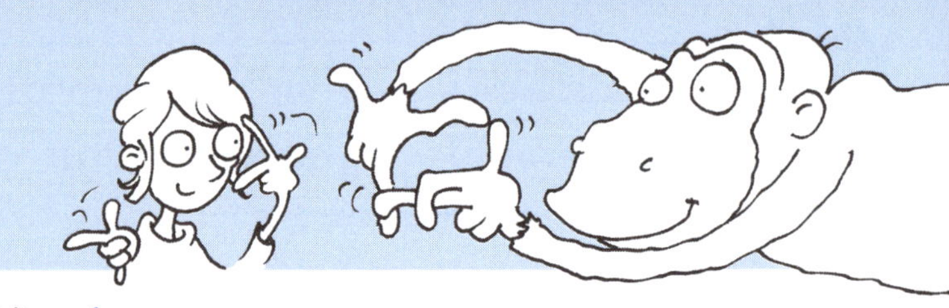

Say Listen Look Understand Remember Practise

del**igh**t	______
midn**igh**t	______
fr**igh**ten	______
fr**igh**tful	______
n**eigh**bour	______
h**eigh**t	______
str**aigh**t	______
en**ough**	______
th**ough**	______
thr**ough**	______
d**augh**ter	______
n**augh**ty	______

1  Write **ei**, **ou** or **au**.

c _ _ gh	w _ _ ght
c _ _ ght	t _ _ ght
en _ _ gh	th _ _ gh
d _ _ ghter	r _ _ gh
t _ _ gh	b _ _ ght
thr _ _ gh	n _ _ ghty
_ _ ght	n _ _ gh

Most verbs show the past tense by adding **ed**.

discover → *discovered*

Irregular verbs have a different form in the past tense.

write → *wrote* *throw* → *threw*

2 Complete the tables.

verb	past tense
buy	
cough	
teach	

verb	past tense
think	
fight	
weigh	

3 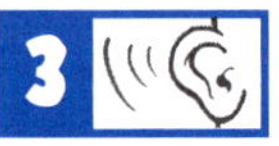 Choose the right word for each space.

tough though through thought

I cut ______ the steak but it was too ______ to chew.

Even ______ it was sunny, I ______ it might rain later.

It was ______ to train the lion to jump ______ the burning hoop.

Spelling Rules! Student Book 3 (ISBN 9780655092605) © Janelle Ho, Helen Pearson

Remember! **Antonyms** are words with the opposite meaning.

day, night   *easy, difficult*   *high, low*

Write a list word that is an antonym.

good ______________   crooked ______________

pleasant ______________   comfort ______________

Proofread this text. The text has eight words that are incorrect. Circle the mistakes. Then write the correct spelling of the words in the boxes.

Our family is very lucky because we have lovely nieghbours. My best freind is there daughter, Lily. Together, we are planning a 'Freight Night' party at my home. We are going to make our home really dark so it feels like midnight. Everyone has to wear a scary costume. If it isn't scary enugh, they have to go through a tunel where we will play a trick on them. I think we'll all have a deelightful time.

6 Write a sentence using each word.

delight (noun) ______________________________

delight (verb) ______________________________

smell (noun) ______________________________

smell (verb) ______________________________

sigh (noun) ______________________________

sigh (verb) ______________________________

Reflection

- I can do this.
- I am not sure.
- I need help.

Elephants can talk to other elephants that are kilometres away using sounds that are too low for humans to hear.

Say Listen Look Understand Remember Practise

laugh	________
toughen	________
graph	________
photograph	________
autograph	________
elephant	________
telephone	________
sphere	________
trophy	________
alphabet	________
phrase	________
physical	________

1 Say each word aloud. Circle the word if **gh** has an **f** sound.

cough	caught	rough
tough	light	laugh
height	enough	weigh
trough	drought	though

2 In text messages and emails, people sometimes write words as they sound, instead of using the correct spelling. Write each word correctly.

coff	larf
________	________
enuff	fone
________	________

3 Divide these list words into syllables. Underline the stressed syllable. Write the number of syllables in each word.

graph	enough	telephone	trophy	physical
○	○	○	○	○
sphere	alphabet	autograph	phrase	laughter
○	○	○	○	○

4 Write the list words in alphabetical order.

____

____

____

Spelling Rules! Student Book 3 (ISBN 9780655092605) © Janelle Ho, Helen Pearson

5 Some words are easier to understand when they are broken up into parts. Use a dictionary to find the meaning of the parts of these words. What other words do you know that start or end this way?

tele = ______________________ + phone = ______________________

The word is ______________________.

photo = ______________________ + graph = ______________________

The word is ______________________.

auto = ______________________ + graph = ______________________

The word is ______________________.

Other words: ____

6 Write list words.

The newspaper article used a ______________ to show that crime rates are falling.

Phil's favourite ______________ is 'rough and ready'.

Mia was awarded the ______________ for the best and fairest player in the netball competition.

When the peels are dried in the sun, they will ______________.

Did you know that Earth is not a perfect ______________?

7 Choose your favourite photograph. Why do you love this photo? Explain why it is meaningful.

____

____

____

____

____

____

____

____

Reflection

I can do this.

I am not sure.

I need help.

Unit

17

No two giraffes have the same pattern on their skin.

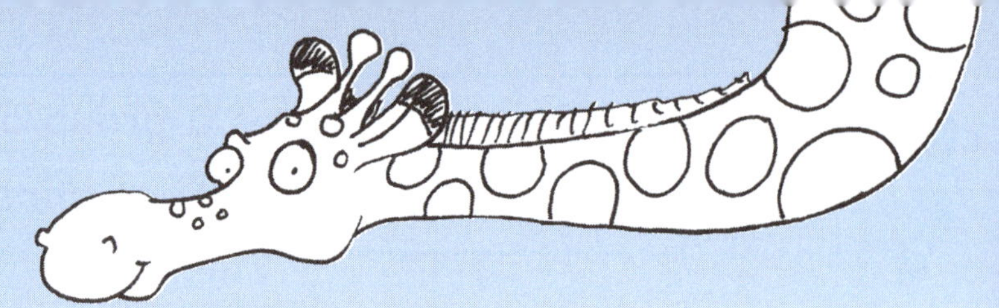

Say Listen Look Understand Remember Practise

puff ____________
cliff ____________
staff ____________
shelf ____________
wolf ____________
scarf ____________
wharf ____________
thief ____________
knife ____________
handkerchief
____
yourself ____________
giraffe ____________

1 Find a list word that rhymes.

calf	laugh	wife
____________	____________	____________
stiff	leaf	bluff
____________	____________	____________

Tip

If a word ends in an **f** sound, has one syllable and a short vowel sound, it usually ends in **ff**.

stuff, off

2 Add a short vowel to make a word.

st _ ff   bl _ ff   sn _ ff   fl _ ff   h _ ff   gr _ ff

Rule

If a noun ends in **f** or **fe**, change the **f** or **fe** to **v** and add **es** to form the plural.   *elf* → *elves*   *life* → *lives*

If a noun ends in **ff** or **ffe**, add **s** to form the plural.

3 Write the plural for each noun.

half ____________	loaf ____________	knife ____________
puff ____________	thief ____________	cliff ____________
yourself ____________	shelf ____________	giraffe ____________

Spelling Rules! Student Book 3 (ISBN 9780655092605) © Janelle Ho, Helen Pearson

A **collective noun** names a group of people, animals or things.

a pod of whales *a fleet of ships* *an army of soldiers*

4 Choose an animal to complete each collective noun. Use a dictionary if you need help.

wolves kittens bees sheep cattle fish

a flock of ____________ a school of ____________

a litter of ____________ a swarm of ____________

a herd of ____________ a pack of ____________

Write one more collective noun: a ______________ of ______________

Make up one yourself: a ______________ of ______________

5 Add a consonant to the beginning of each word to make a new word that rhymes.

ring ⟶ bring

_ lane _ room _ rain _ row _ pace

_ rust _ lace _ low _ rush _ win

6 Write an antonym for each clue.

A		K								
B			L							
C				H						
D					R					
E						T				
F							T			
G								Y		
H									L	
I										Y

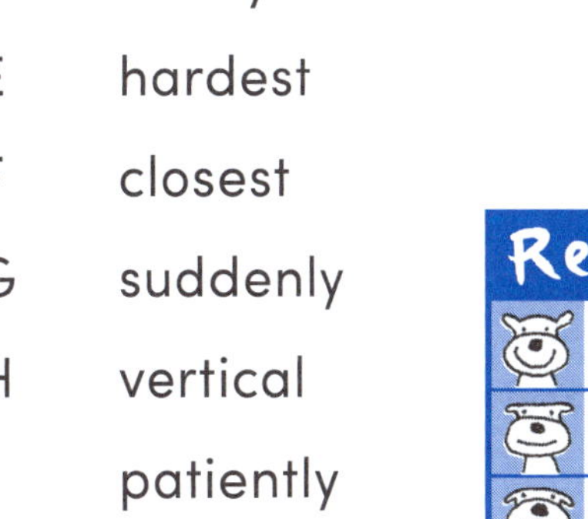

A answer

B freeze

C throw

D safety

E hardest

F closest

G suddenly

H vertical

I patiently

Reflection

I can do this.

I am not sure.

I need help.

Our planet Earth is not a perfect **sphere**. It is a little flat at the poles and bulges a little around the equator.

Fill in the missing vowels.

w _ _ ght

b _ _ ght

g _ _ nt

c _ _ ght

mosq _ _ t _

Fill in the missing consonants.

ni _ _ t

s _ a _ _

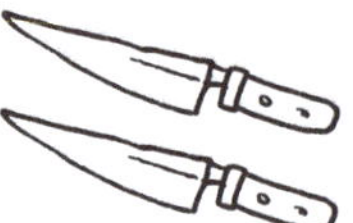

_ _ i _ es

t _ o _ _ y

_ _ ie _

Complete the tables.

singular	plural
graph	
	trophies
trolley	
	queues

singular	plural
cliff	
	shelves
wharf	
	wolves

Complete the tables.

	guide	laugh	frighten	squeal
add ed				
add ing				

	puff	receive	brag	swallow
add ed				
add ing				

5 Write the homophone for each word.

raw	site	threw	weight	write
______	______	______	______	______
fort	choose	wade	cord	stares
______	______	______	______	______

6 Circle the words that are not used correctly in this story.

Last holidays, Mum bought cheep tickets to Singapore. The flight took ate hours and I had red most of my book by the time the plain landed. I couldn't sleep because as soon as we took of, a baby sitting only too rose behind us started to cry. She didn't give her parents a moment of piece the hole journey.

The whether their was hot and sticky every day, so Mum decided we should all by some knew summer clothes. When we packed to go home, our suitcase was so full I thought it might brake. It was not a problem, though, because we through out for pears of old jeans to make room.

In a polysyllabic word (a word with more than one syllable), one syllable is said louder than the others. This is the **stressed syllable**.
A monosyllabic word (a word with only one syllable) is always considered a stressed syllable.
The schwa only occurs in an unstressed syllable.

7 Say each word. Underline the stressed syllable.

mountain chemical refuse September elephant enough

8 Each word contains the schwa. Write the letter(s) that represent the sound.

geni_____s _____wake qui_____t for_____gn physic_____l

Unit 19

Snakes use their tongues to smell.

Say Listen Look Understand Remember Practise	
wrinkle	______
wrestle	______
knead	______
knowledge	______
gnaw	______
gnome	______
hour	______
honest	______
island	______
tongue	______
doubt	______
ghost	______

1 Circle the silent letter in each of these words. Write a list word with the same silent letter.

gnaw ______	hour ______
debt ______	listen ______
wrong ______	ghoul ______
rogue ______	knock ______

2 These body parts all have silent letters. Write the word.

______

______

______

______

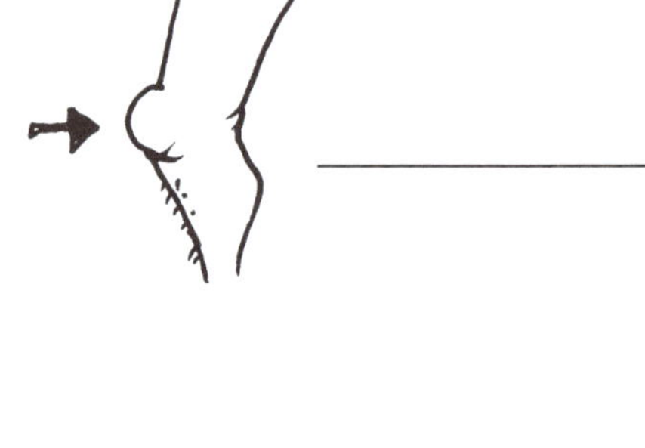

______

3 Add a suffix to each word. Circle the silent letter.

ghost + ly ______

wrap + ed ______

doubt + ful ______

gnaw + ing ______

wrinkle + ing ______

honest + y ______

Spelling Rules! Student Book 3 (ISBN 9780655092605) © Janelle Ho, Helen Pearson

Some letters can't start or end words.

- No English words begin with double consonants.
- No English words end with **q** or **v**.

These words have all come from another language. That is why the spelling looks unusual. Match each type of boat to its description. The first one has been done for you.

canoe (Spanish)	a boat with sails
kayak (Inuit)	a very small rowboat
yacht (Dutch)	a small boat with a roof made of mats
pontoon (French)	a light boat with a cover that fits around the paddler's waist
gondola (Italian)	a boat with two joined hulls
catamaran (Tamil)	a lightweight boat with paddles
dinghy (Hindi)	a boat used to support a temporary bridge
sampan (Chinese)	a long flat-bottomed boat with one oar

There are many words you can use instead of *went*.
The dog wriggled through the narrow gap in the fence.
Find a better word than *went* to complete these sentences.

The ghost ____________ through the door.

The elephant ____________ through the reeds to reach the waterhole.

Jack and Jill ____________ up the hill to fetch a pail of water.

We ____________ through the dark tunnel.

Fill in the missing vowels to make words you can use instead of *walked*.
Add four of your own. Use two of these verbs in your own sentences.

str _ d _   d _ wdl _ d   t _ pt _ _ d   w _ ddl _ d   tr _ dg _ d

____

____

____

____

Unit 20

Cows can fall **a**sleep standing up.

Say **L**isten **L**ook **U**nderstand **R**emember **P**ractise

across	____________
always	____________
about	____________
around	____________
almost	____________
already	____________
ahead	____________
asleep	____________
above	____________
another	____________
along	____________
altogether	____________

1 Write a list word that means the opposite.

behind ____________

below ____________

separately ____________

never ____________

awake ____________

2 Colour the circle if the **a** at the beginning is a schwa. Underline the stressed syllable.

alive	◯	after	◯
again	◯	along	◯
almost	◯	away	◯
across	◯	alike	◯
always	◯	aloud	◯

3 Arrange these words from least often to most often.

sometimes always often never rarely

____

4 Write list words.

This pen doesn't work. Can you pass me ____________ one?

We started our sport lesson by running ____________ the oval.

Hurry up! It's ____________ two o'clock.

My cat can walk ____________ the top of the fence.

We rowed ____________ the river for a picnic.

A long path is not the same as *along the path*.
Remember to leave a space between each word in a sentence.

5 Write these sentences, leaving spaces between each word.

Donotbeafraid. ____________________

Mybrotherisawaysicktoday. ____________________

Jackisaloneinthehouse. ____________________

Mytwinsisterslike todressalike. ____________________

6 Write two letters that are the end of one word and the beginning of another. Write both words. An example has been done for you.

almo _ _ ep	almost	step
abo _ _ ry	________	________
thi _ _ fect	________	________
sche _ _ ssy	________	________
gui _ _ cide	________	________
monar _ _ oose	________	________

A **preposition** is a word that shows where an object is in relation to another object.
My bag is under the table.
The list words *across*, *about*, *around* and *above* are prepositions.

7 Describe a room in your home. Use prepositions to help your reader imagine the position of objects in the room.

____

____

____

____

____

____

____

Unit 21

When you sneeze, air and snot fly out of your nose at 160 km/h. **Dis**gusting!

Say Listen Look Understand Remember Practise

untidy	________
unlikely	________
mischief	________
misplace	________
misbehave	________
mistake	________
disagree	________
disgrace	________
disgusting	________
dishonest	________
disobey	________
discover	________

Tip

A **prefix** is added at the beginning of a word. It makes a new word that is different in meaning.

1 Add **un**, **mis** or **dis** as a prefix.

____lucky	____agree
____behave	____safe
____healthy	____honest
____appear	____understand
____obey	____tidy
____place	____true
____likely	____like

Tip

The prefixes **un** and **dis** both give a word an opposite meaning.

kind → *unkind*

approve → *disapprove*

2 Give each sentence the opposite meaning by adding **un** or **dis**.

The sun appeared over the horizon.

____

Your desk is so tidy!

____

Sam really likes pumpkin.

____

I agree with you.

____

The train is likely to arrive on time.

____

Spelling Rules! Student Book 3 (ISBN 9780655092605) © Janelle Ho, Helen Pearson

Synonyms are words with the same meaning.
Small and *little* are synonyms.

3 Find list words that are synonyms for these words.

error ________________ find ________________

lose ________________ messy ________________

gross ________________ trouble ________________

4 Jarrad's bedroom is a mess. Describe each object using an adjective that rhymes with the clue. Then use a list word to comment on the mess.

Jarrad's shiny bike helmet is on the floor. How untidy!
(tiny)

His __________ socks are under the bed. How ____________!
(jelly)

His __________ football is on his pillow. What a ____________!
(thirty)

His __________ jacket is hanging behind the door. How ____________!
(blue)

When you add a **prefix**, do not remove any letters. If the prefix ends in the same letter the base word starts with, keep both letters.

un + noticed → unnoticed
dis + similar → dissimilar

5 Write the prefix and the base word.

misspell = _____ + ____________ unnoticeable = _____ + ______________

unnecessary = ____ + ______________ misshape = _____ + ____________

dissatisfied = _____ + _____________ unnamed = _____ + _____________

6 Use your dictionary to find the word meanings. Use both words in one sentence.

dismay	____
mishap	____

Unit 22

New South Wales is made up of around 70 different First Nations, each with their own language or language group.

Say Listen Look Understand Remember Practise

country	____________
state	____________
northern	____________
western	____________
south	____________
capital	____________
territory	____________
Australia	____________
New South Wales	____________
Victoria	____________
Tasmania	____________
Queensland	____________

1 You have written a letter to your school principal. Follow the example and address the envelope correctly.

Ms R Smith
Rosehill State School
16 Howard Street
Rosehill, Tasmania 4981

____
____
____
____

2 Fill in the missing letters. Make sure each word begins with a capital letter.

_e_ _o_ _h _a_ _s N_ _th_ _n T_ _ri_ory

_ic_ _ _i_ S_ _t_ _u_ _r_ _ _ _

T_ _ _a_ _ _ W_ _ _er_ _ _s_ _a_ _ _

Q_e_ _s_ _ _d _ _ _t_ _l_ _n C_pi_ _l _er_ _t_ _y

3 Join each capital city to its state or territory.

Melbourne	Western Australia	Sydney	Northern Territory
Perth	Tasmania	Brisbane	New South Wales
Hobart	South Australia	Darwin	Australian Capital Territory
Adelaide	Victoria	Canberra	Queensland

Spelling Rules! Student Book 3 (ISBN 9780655092605) © Janelle Ho, Helen Pearson

4 Choose a word to fit each space.

northern
eastern
southern
western

Brisbane and Sydney are ______________ capitals.

The most ______________ capital is Hobart.

Perth is the most ______________ capital, while the most ______________ capital is Darwin.

5 The days of the week are all proper nouns. Write the days in order.

______________ was the day of the sun.

______________ was the day of the moon.

______________ was Tiw's day. Tiw was the Norse god of war.

______________ was Woden's day. Woden was the chief Norse god.

______________ was Thor's day. Thor was the Norse god of thunder.

______________ was Frigga's day. Frigga was the chief Norse goddess.

______________ was Saturn's day. Saturn was the Roman god of farming.

Apostrophes can show that someone owns something.

Tim's bag.

6 Use the person's name and **'s** to show who owns each object.

The book belongs to Ari. It is ______________.

The coat belongs to Pia. It is ______________.

The shoes belong to Steve. They are ______________.

The scarf belongs to Mum. It is ______________.

7 Circle the letters that should be written as capitals.

cassie goes to epping for gym training every friday.

the tasman sea separates australia and new zealand.

captain cook's ship was called endeavour.

Reflection

- I can do this.
- I am not sure.
- I need help.

Unit 23

Playing a **yidaki** can help you breathe better! **Deadly**!

Say Listen Look Understand Remember Practise	
Mob	______
Elder	______
Aunty	______
Uncle	______
deadly	______
gammon	______
tucker	______
humpy	______
yakka	______
yidaki	______
boomerang	______
marngrook	______

1 Write the list words in alphabetical order.

______ ______ ______

______ ______ ______

______ ______ ______

______ ______ ______

2 Say each list word. Write the words that answer the questions.

Which word has one syllable? ______

Which words have three syllables?

______ ______

Which words begin with a vowel sound?

______ ______ ______

Tip

Some words can be written in both lower case and upper case (capital letters). *aunty* *Aunty* *uncle* *Uncle*

When a word is written with a capital letter, it is part of a name or is important in the community.

3 Choose a word to fill each gap. Write the plural.

Mob	Elder	Aunty	Uncle

Aboriginal people belong to ______. Each Mob is linked to a place or Country. The ______ are responsible for teaching the stories of their people. They are made up of respected women and men in the community. They are known as ______ and ______.

Spelling Rules! Student Book 3 (ISBN 9780655092605) © Janelle Ho, Helen Pearson

4 Write a list word.

________________ ________________

________________ ________________

________________ ________________

5 Use the clues to write a list word.

very good ________________ fake or pretend ________________

food ________________ temporary shelter ________________

respected member of an Aboriginal community ________________

6 Add **er** or **est**.

The Aboriginal peoples have the ____________ (old) culture in the world.

Uluru is the ____________ (large) rock monolith in the world.

Did you know that Darwin is both the ____________ (sunny) and ____________ (wet) city in Australia?

Tip Some **adjectives** change when you use them to compare different things.

good → better → best   *bad → worse → worst*

7 Choose the word that fits each sentence.

I am good at high jump but I'm ____________ at long jump.

I am bad at breast stroke but I'm ____________ at backstroke.

Osman sang a solo at the concert as he is the ____________ singer in our class.

I don't like it when my sister makes dinner. She is the ____________ cook I know.

8 The adjective *nice* is used too often. Find a better word for each sentence.

My cousin is very nice. ________________

This cake is nice. ________________

Reflection

I can do this.

I am not sure.

I need help.

The biggest frog in the world is the Goliath frog. A Goliath frog can weigh as much as a house cat!

1 These words all have one or two prefixes or suffixes. Write the base words to which the prefixes or suffixes are added. Underline the prefixes and suffixes.

knives ______________	littlest ______________	burrowed ______________
weirder ______________	guessing ______________	disappear ______________
returned ______________	bravely ______________	replied ______________
beginning ______________	unhealthy ______________	misbehaving ______________

2 Choose a word to fit each space.

above	another	across	around	almost	already

Tim's best friend is Sandra, who lives ______________ the road. They play together ______________ every day. Last weekend they went to the park to play cricket. Sandra kept hitting the ball high ______________ Tim's head. He had to run a long way after it. Tim asked his older brother Toby to be fielder so he wouldn't have to keep running ______________ after the ball. Sandra hit the next ball high in the air and Toby caught it!

'Give me ______________ chance, will you?' asked Sandra.

The boys laughed and said it was now her turn to get some exercise. They had ______________ run a long way!

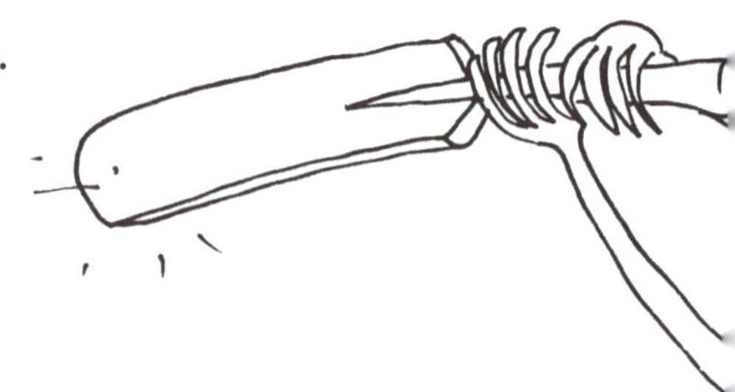

3 Fill in the missing vowels.

bel _ _ ve	disapp _ _ nt	fr _ _ nd	disapp _ _ r
disagr _ _	misch _ _ f	qu _ _ tly	f _ _ rce
empt _ _ d	l _ _ dly	p _ _ ceful	_ _ str _ l _ a

Spelling Rules! Student Book 3 (ISBN 9780655092605) © Janelle Ho, Helen Pearson

4 Add a letter to the beginning of each word to make a new word.

_ lean	_ nail	_ rail	_ tone	_ room
_ rain	_ lower	_ new	_ now	_ rush
_ heat	_ harm	_ rack	_ rust	_ lack

5 Circle the letters that should be written as capitals. Add capital letters and apostrophes.

my name is ahmed and im afraid of snakes. i live in alice springs and i know there are plenty of snakes out there.

last sunday i was sitting outside reading charlottes web by e.b white. mum called me and i looked up. there it was. a python. mum is a vet and is used to handling snakes. she picked up the python and popped it into my brothers gym bag. i breathed again. its a good thing she was home.

6 Match the capital city to its traditional place name.

Canberra	Yuggera
Melbourne	Nipaluna
Brisbane	Eora
Darwin	Larrakia
Sydney	Ngunnawal
Hobart	Woiworung
Perth	Wajuk

7 Use your dictionary.

What is the next word after stork?

____

What is the word before toast?

____

Arrange in alphabetical order:
strong, stale, stink, stupid, stage

______________ ______________

______________ ______________

____

Unit 25

Meerkats are very help**ful** animals. They often take care of each other's babies.

Say Listen Look Understand Remember Practise

harm**ful** ______
peace**ful** ______
colour**ful** ______
grate**ful** ______
boast**ful** ______
plenti**ful** ______
beauti**ful** ______
help**less** ______
use**less** ______
care**less** ______
fear**less** ______
life**less** ______

1 Add the suffix.

joy, cheer, watch, use, peace → ful

______
______
______
______
______

care, hope, blame, help, harm → less

______
______
______
______
______

Tip The suffixes **ful** and **less** usually make the new words **antonyms**. Antonyms are words that are opposite in meaning.

2 Make antonyms.

use	______	______	care	______	______
harm	______	______	pain	______	______
colour	______	______	joy	______	______

3 Some words add **ful** but not **less**. Circle these in blue. Others add **less** but not **ful**. Circle these in red.

play	life	blame	plenty
boast	beauty	face	hand

Spelling Rules! Student Book 3 (ISBN 9780655092605) © Janelle Ho, Helen Pearson

If a word ends in **y**, change **y** to **i** before adding **ful** or **less**.

duty → dutiful

4 Write the word.

mercy + ful → ____________ fancy + ful → ____________

pity + less → ____________ penny + less → ____________

5 Use the clue to find a list word to fit each sentence.

I sprained my ankle because I was ____________. (not paying attention)

Aunty was ____________ in facing the bullies. (brave)

'Thank you! I am ____________ you could help.' (glad)

Belle's description of her character was ____________ so she rewrote it. (dull)

We were shocked when a fight broke out on our ____________ street. (quiet)

The singer was so ____________ about his success that he lost many fans. (praising oneself)

Chocolate is ____________ to dogs. (dangerous)

6 Words for quantities sometimes end in **ful**. *Handful* is an example. Use the pictures to help you complete the list of ingredients.

To make a pancake, you need the following ingredients:

1 ____________ of flour

2 ____________ of baking powder

1 egg

1 ____________ of milk

2 ____________ of oil

7 Write your own sentence using these words.

awful	____________
wonderful	____________

Reflection

- I can do this.
- I am not sure.
- I need help.

Unit 26

Sharks can't swim back**wards**.

Say Listen Look Understand Remember Practise	
kind**ness**	______
happi**ness**	______
revis**ion**	______
televis**ion**	______
direct**ion**	______
friend**ship**	______
king**dom**	______
free**dom**	______
for**wards**	______
back**wards**	______
child**hood**	______
neighbour**hood**	
______	

1 Make nouns by choosing the right suffix to add to these words.

ness ship dom hood

kind______	friend______
king______	late______
dark______	loud______
child______	truthful______
bore______	free______
neighbour______	tired______
forgetful______	sponsor______
gentle______	adult______

If a word ends in **y**, change the **y** to **i** before adding **ness**.

lonely → *loneliness*

2 Add **ness** to these words.

happy	lazy	empty
______	______	______
ugly	friendly	dizzy
______	______	______

3 Name each mathematical operation. Each one ends in **ion**.

2 + 3 = 5 ______	6 − 2 = 4 ______
4 × 2 = 8 ______	6 ÷ 3 = 2 ______

Some verbs can be changed into nouns by adding **ion**.

If the verb ends in **e**, drop the **e** before adding **ion**.

confuse → confusion

4 Complete the tables.

verb	noun
act	
	separation
discuss	
	revision
connect	

verb	noun
	introduction
direct	
	explanation
televise	
	starvation

5 The suffix **wards** means *in the direction of*. Write four words that use this suffix and give the antonym for each one.

		word	antonym
in		______	______
for	wards	______	______
up		______	______

6 Make a noun by adding a suffix to the adjective. Look in a dictionary. Use both nouns in one sentence.

wise
likely

______

______

The words **revision** and **television** have the same root, **vision**, which comes from the Latin word that means *to see*.

7 What do **re** and **tele** mean?

re: ______

tele: ______

Reflection

- I can do this.
- I am not sure.
- I need help.

Unit 27

The world's smallest frog is from Cuba. It is just 8.5 **milli**metres long.

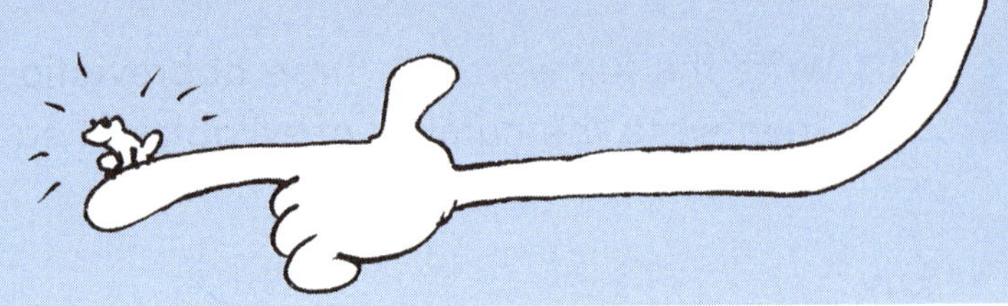

Say Listen Look Understand Remember Practise

metre ____________
kilometre ____________
centimetre ____________
millimetre ____________
litre ____________
gram ____________
decade ____________
uniform ____________
bicycle ____________
triangle ____________
dozen ____________
dollar ____________

1 Write the list word that is most appropriate for measuring each quantity.

weight of an orange ____________
distance between cities ____________
cost of a bus ride ____________
height of a person ____________
quantity of water ____________
length of a ruler ____________
length of an ant ____________
number of eggs ____________

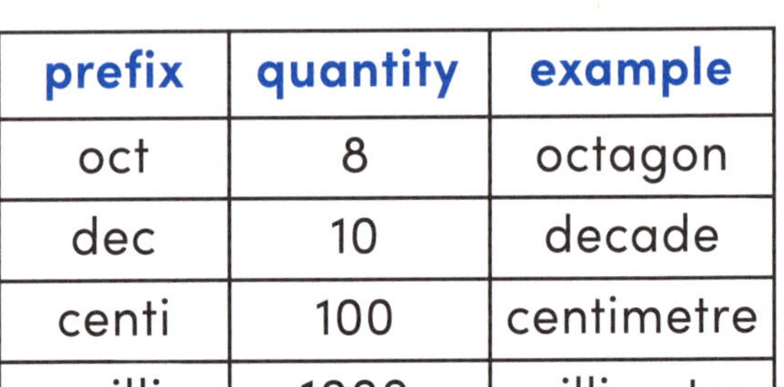

Tip Some prefixes indicate quantity.

prefix	quantity	example
uni	1	unicycle
bi	2	biplane
tri	3	tricycle
quadr	4	quarter

prefix	quantity	example
oct	8	octagon
dec	10	decade
centi	100	centimetre
milli	1000	millimetre

2 Choose a word ending for each prefix.

pede form agon uple cycle opus imal angle

uni____________ bi____________ tri____________ quadr____________

oct____________ dec____________ oct____________ milli____________

Spelling Rules! Student Book 3 (ISBN 9780655092698) © Janelle Ho, Helen Pearson

3 Write the full word for these abbreviations and symbols. Then write the number of syllables in each word in the circle.

km ______________ ○

mm ______________ ○

mL ______________ ○

g ______________ ○

cm ______________ ○

L ______________ ○

kg ______________ ○

$ ______________ ○

4 Write as many words as you can starting with each prefix. A dictionary will help.

uni 1	bi 2	tri 3

5 The letters of most of these words have been jumbled up. Write the sentences correctly.

I ma het olny mebmer of my faimly bron tihs cnetruy.

____

We hnug ornage rtinagles on eth fecnes to mrak het tarck.

____

6 An idiom is a saying that is used and understood by a group of people. Write the meaning of this idiom.

baker's dozen ______________________________

____

Reflection

- I can do this.
- I am not sure.
- I need help.

Unit 28

The 'running man' **exit** sign was designed by Yukio Ota in 1979.

Say **L**isten **L**ook **U**nderstand **R**emember **P**ractise

exit ______
extra ______
expert ______
experience ______
extreme ______
example ______
exact ______
excuse ______
excellent ______
exclaim ______
excite ______
exercise ______

1 Say each list word. Sort them according to the number of syllables.

2 syllables	3 syllables	4 syllables
______	______	______
______	______	
______	______	
______		
______		
______		
______		
______		

2 **in** is a prefix that can mean 'not'. Add **in** to the words.

in + experience ______
in + active ______
in + valid ______
in + sane ______
in + exact ______
in + justice ______

3 Add suffixes to each word.

exit
+ s ______
+ ed ______
+ ing ______

extreme
+ ly ______

exact
+ ed ______
+ ly ______

excite
+ s ______
+ ed ______
+ ed + ly ______

Spelling Rules! Student Book 3 (ISBN 9780655092605) © Janelle Ho, Helen Pearson

Circle the word if **c** makes a soft sound as in *cent*.

exact excuse cyclone exclaim excite exercise

Why does **c** make a soft sound? ______

______

Write a list word for each clue.

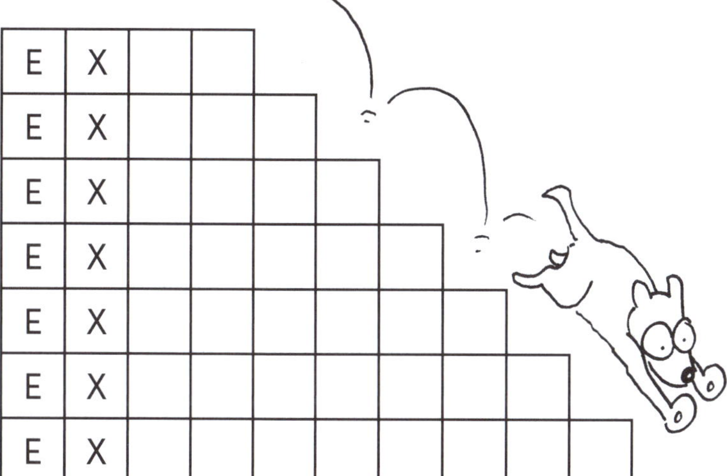

E	X								
E	X								
E	X								
E	X								
E	X								
E	X								
E	X								

way out

more than needed

one who knows a lot about a subject

cry out in surprise

physical activity

very good

something that happens to you

Instead of using *extremely + adjective*, use a word that says it all. One example is given. Use a thesaurus to find another. Then write with one of the words.

	Example	**Your word**	**Sentence**
extremely loud	noisy		
extremely big	gigantic		
extremely cold	frosty		
extremely quiet	calm		

What do you excel at?

______

______

______

______

Reflection

I can do this.

I am not sure.

I need help.

Unit 29

Only female mosquitoes suck blood.

Say Listen Look Understand Remember Practise

hero ____________
piano ____________
zero ____________
radio ____________
toe ____________
canoe ____________
kangaroo ____________
taboo ____________
sofa ____________
drama ____________
idea ____________
era ____________

If a noun ends in **o**, you usually add **es** to make the plural.

echo → echoes

If the word comes from another language, you usually add **s** to make the plural.

avocado (Spanish) → avocados

piano (Italian) → pianos

If the word ends in two vowels, just add **s**.

radio → radios

Write the plural ending for these nouns.

canoe___	mosquito___	hero___
kimono___	radio___	toe___
volcano___	kangaroo___	dingo___
video___	banjo___	studio___

Write the plural ending for the items on this list.

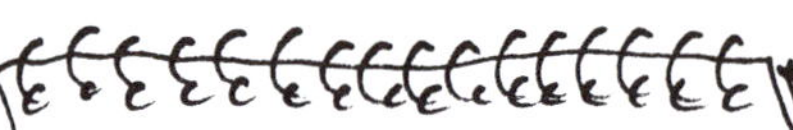

3 kg potato___
1 kg tomato___
2 mango___
2 avocado___
0.5 kg pea___
4 banana___
4 peach___

An abbreviation is a short form of a longer word. Use your dictionary to find the longer word for each abbreviation.

hippo ____________
rhino ____________
photo ____________
kilo ____________

Spelling Rules! Student Book 3 (ISBN 9780655092605) © Janelle Ho, Helen Pearson

4 Why is there no singular form for these words?

scissors tongs pliers trousers binoculars tweezers

All the words ______________________________

____

5 Complete the tables.

singular	plural
woman	
	mice
salmon	
	eras
cockroach	

singular	plural
photo	
	people
tooth	
	magpies
idea	

Take care with these words.

there = a place (<u>here</u> and t<u>here</u>)

their = belonging to them (It is always followed by a noun.)

they're = they are

Where are their clothes? They're over there!

6 Write your own sentences to show how each word is used.

there ______________________________

____

their ______________________________

____

____

they're ______________________________

____

____

Unit 30 Revision

In English, the **w**riting goes from left to right. In Arabic, the **w**riting goes from right to left. In Japanese, the **w**riting goes from top to bottom, in columns.

 1 Fill in the missing letters.

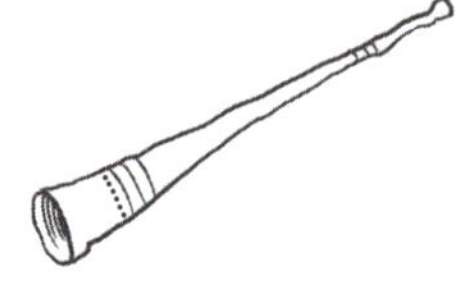

can_ _   r_d_ _   tr_ _ _g_ _   b_c_ _le   y_da_ _

 2 Complete the tables.

adjective	adverb
quiet	
extreme	
	funnily
	beautifully

noun	adjective
	free
happiness	
	gentle
doubt	

Holy adjectives… It's the homophone!

3 Write the homophone for each word.

there ____________   fore ____________
hole ____________   brake ____________
peace ____________   write ____________
night ____________   stair ____________
steel ____________   threw ____________
blue ____________   rap ____________
new ____________   guessed ____________
fort ____________   allowed ____________
wait ____________   eight ____________

4 Use the clues to make a new word.

thought + 2 suffixes ____________________ excite + 2 suffixes ____________________

friend + 1 prefix + 1 suffix ________________________

agree + 1 prefix + 1 suffix ________________________

Write your own.

kind ____________________ ____________________

know ____________________ ____________________

Tip

Antonyms are words with the opposite meaning. *Big* and *little* are antonyms. Antonyms are also formed using prefixes and suffixes.

kind ***un****kind* *harm****ful*** *harm****less***

5 Write an antonym for each of these words.

hard ________________ entrance ________________ active ________________

tidy ________________ end ________________ painful ________________

question ________________ ugly ________________ honest ________________

6 Homographs have the same spelling but more than one meaning. Give two meanings for each of these words.

cricket 1. ______________________________ 2. ______________________________

pupil 1. ______________________________ 2. ______________________________

coach 1. ______________________________ 2. ______________________________

match 1. ______________________________ 2. ______________________________

7 Write a word beginning with **ex**. You may need to add a suffix.

What's your ________________ for being late?

The builder needs ________________ measurements for all the rooms.

Dad likes to ________________ in the morning while Mum likes to do it in the evenings.

The teacher provided an ________________ ________________ of a well-written text.

I'm very ______________ about interviewing an ________________ on the corrobore frog.

Unit 31

The first living creature to go on a space mission was Laika the dog, in 1957.

Say Listen Look Understand Remember Practise	
station	______
fiction	______
section	______
fraction	______
cushion	______
fashion	______
mission	______
expression	______
religion	______
million	______
champion	______
information	______

1 Write list words.

A millionaire has a ______ dollars.

I'll meet you at the train ______.

I am going to be a ______ swimmer.

One quarter is a ______.

I'd like to be an astronaut on a space ______ to Mars.

Bring a ______ to sit on.

Buddhism is a major ______ in Asia.

I can tell from her ______ that the orange is sour.

2 Would you look in the fiction or non-fiction section for these books?

A History of Our Nation *non-fiction section*

Life on a Space Station ______

Charlie Cheers the Champions ______

The Pyramids of Ancient Egypt ______

3 Write a list word to match each shape.

Spelling Rules! Student Book 3 (ISBN 9780655092605) © Janelle Ho, Helen Pearson

4 There has been a word explosion. Find a noun to match each verb.

verb	noun
imagine	
explore	
infect	
prepare	
operate	
organise	
explain	
separate	

5 Find the **ion** words in the trophy and write them in the **suffix added** column. Write the verb that belongs to the same word family as the noun.

mountaincertainiron
suspicionmusician
curtainininformationjoin
maintaincontainexplosion
decisionaim

Base word (verb)	Suffix added
______________	______________
______________	______________
______________	______________
______________	______________

6 Write these fractions as words.

$\frac{1}{2}$ ______________________

$\frac{1}{4}$ ______________________

7 Use both rhyming words in one sentence.

fashion passion

____

____

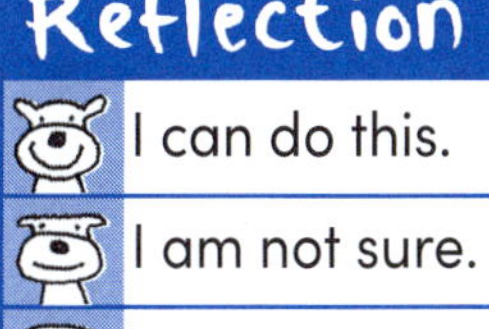

Unit 32

The first water treat**ment** happened in the 1700s. People used wool, sponge and charcoal.

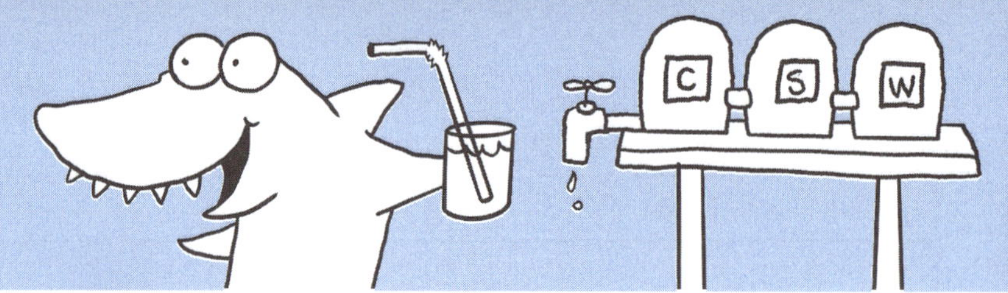

Say **L**isten **L**ook **U**nderstand **R**emember **P**ractise

move**ment**	______
state**ment**	______
argu**ment**	______
amaze**ment**	______
measure**ment**	______
govern**ment**	______
environ**ment**	______
treat**ment**	______
develop**ment**	______
attach**ment**	______
encourage**ment**	______
disappoint**ment**	______

Tip **ment** changes a verb to a noun.

1 Write the list words as base word + **ment**.

treatment → treat + ______

development → ______ + ment

attachment → ______ + ______

movement → ______ + ______

statement → ______ + ______

amazement → ______ + ______

government → ______ + ______

measurement → ______ + ______

encouragement → ______ + ______

disappointment → ______ + ______

environment → ______ + ______

2 Say each list word. Write the words that match the number of syllables.

2 syllables

______

______

______

4 syllables

______

______

______

______

3 Add suffixes to **move**.

move + s ______

move + ed ______

move + ing ______

move + er ______

move + ment ______

Which spelling rule does not apply when **s** and **ment** are added? Why not?

______

______

4 Each group of words forms a category. Write a list word for each category and add more examples.

Category	Examples
____________	minister, parliament, MP, __________, __________
____________	hours, metres, grams, __________, __________
____________	erosion, recycling, pollution, __________, __________

5 Synonyms are words that have the same meaning. Write a list word that is a synonym.

1. growth
2. cheer
3. care
4. quarrel
5. surroundings
6. declaration

Hidden word: ________________

Tip Prefixes and suffixes are types of affixes.

6 Add as many affixes as you can.

treat: ________________________

attach: ________________________

develop: ________________________

7 The words *amazement* and *disappointment* describe feelings. Describe a time when you felt one of these feelings.

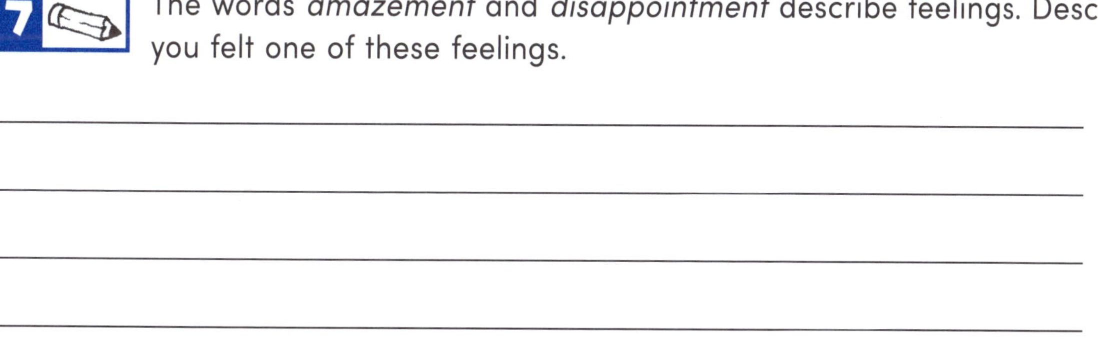

Unit 33

Augie the world-record-holding dog is cap**able** of holding how many tennis balls in his mouth?

a three
b five
c twelve

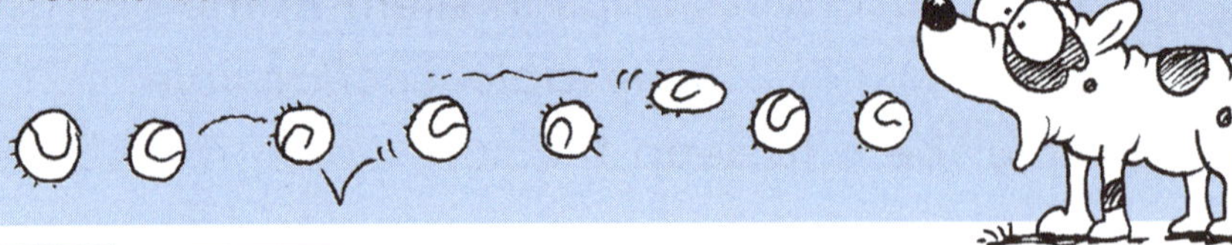

Say Listen Look Understand Remember Practise

reli**able**	______
cap**able**	______
ador**able**	______
avail**able**	______
comfort**able**	______
miser**able**	______
valu**able**	______
horr**ible**	______
terr**ible**	______
sens**ible**	______
flex**ible**	______
respons**ible**	______

1 Add **ible** or **able** to make a list word.

reli______ sens______
respons______ flex______
ador______ terr______
cap______ miser______
comfort______ valu______

2 Draw a line to match each adjective to its meaning. Use a dictionary if you need help.

edible	able to be carried
visible	able to be heard
legible	able to be bent
audible	able to be eaten
portable	able to be seen
inflatable	able to be read
flexible	able to be filled with air

Rule

Adverbs tell us more about verbs. They often end in **ly**.
When you add **ly** to a word ending in **able** or **ible**, change **le** to **ly**.
valuable → *valuably*
horrible → *horribly*

3 Add **ly** to make the adverb.

adjective	**adverb**
	reliably
valuable	
	capably
comfortable	
	terribly
invisible	
miserable	
responsible	

Spelling Rules! Student Book 3 (ISBN 9780655092605) © Janelle Ho, Helen Pearson

If the base word ends in silent **e**, the **e** is usually dropped before adding **ible** or **able**. *believable* *collapsible*
Keep the **e** to keep the soft **c** or soft **g** sound. *noticeable* *changeable*

4 Change each verb to an adjective by adding **able**.

desire ____________________

admire ____________________

forgive ____________________

notice ____________________

consider ____________________

profit ____________________

5 Change each verb to an adjective by adding **ible**.

response ____________________

sense ____________________

collapse ____________________

submerse ____________________

reverse ____________________

flex ____________________

6 Add a suitable adjective that ends in **able** or **ible**.

a ____________________ chair

an ____________________ journey

a ____________________ nappy

a ____________________ friend

an ____________________ baby

a ____________________ shock

a ____________________ seatbelt

a ____________________ organiser

7 Add the prefix **un**, **in** or **im** to the word in brackets to make the antonym.

The old sofa was very ____________________. (comfortable)

Yusef is ____________________ of seeing a ball without throwing or kicking it. (capable)

During a storm, our wi-fi connection can be ____________________. (reliable)

Did you know that it is ____________________ to lick your own elbow? (possible)

The support the team received was ____________________. (credible)

The voice on the other end of the phone was ____________________. (mistakable)

Answer: b

Unit 34

The largest **pizza** ever baked measured 37.4 metres in diameter.

Say Listen Look Understand Remember Practise

igloo ______
robot ______
yacht ______
iceberg ______
khaki ______
tsunami ______
kindergarten ______
kowtow ______
pizza ______
spaghetti ______
chocolate ______
restaurant ______

1 Here are some Italian words. Which ones can you eat? Which ones can you drink?

cappuccino latte pizza spaghetti zucchini broccoli risotto gelato

Eat: ______

______

Drink: ______

______

2 Find a list word that fits each meaning. Write the word again.

_ _ _ o _ An Inuit (Eskimo) word meaning *house* ______

_ h _ k _ A Hindi (Indian) word meaning *dusty* ______

_ s _ _ a _ _ A Japanese word meaning *harbour wave* ______

_ i _ d _ _ g _ _ t _ _ A German word meaning *child's garden* ______

k _ _ _ _ _ A Chinese word meaning *bow deeply* ______

_ o _ _ _ A Czech word meaning *slave* ______

3 Write the correct word.

cacao cocoa chocolate

______ and ______ come from beans that grow on ______ trees.

Spelling Rules! Student Book 3 (ISBN 9780655092605) © Janelle Ho, Helen Pearson

4 Write the list word you might find in these locations. Try to use a different list word for each.

The Antarctic Ocean ____________________

A factory handling dangerous chemicals ____________________

A large lake ____________________

A school ____________________

At a restaurant ____________________

The Arctic ____________________

Tip **Desert** and **dessert** are often confused, even though they are not homophones.

desert = hot, dry place

dessert = sweet food

I'd like a second serve of dessert!

5 Colour the correct word.

It is often cold at night in the | desert | dessert |.

My favourite | desert | dessert | is jelly and ice-cream.

6 Colour the correct homophone.

We used a | course | coarse | sieve to remove the small pebbles.

Dad has just finished a training | course | coarse | for cricket umpires.

7 Write a paragraph about eating a meal in a restaurant.
Use these words: *restaurant, menu, course.*

____

____

____

____

____

____

____

Reflection

- I can do this.
- I am not sure.
- I need help.

Some experts say the average adult speaks 12 500 words a day.

1 Make a new word by adding a letter.

save	______	(cut off beard)	piece	______	(stick into)
hose	______	(an animal)	word	______	(Earth)
steam	______	(small river)	truck	______	(hit)
quit	______	(bed cover)	treat	______	(warning)

2 Make a new word by removing a letter.

though	______	(strong)	grain	______	(get more)
violent	______	(colour)	learn	______	(slant or bend)
craft	______	(it floats)	barrow	______	(goes with a bow)
brain	______	(healthy food)	thread	______	(trample)

3 Change one letter to make a new word.

suction	______	(a part)	worm	______	(group of letters)
green	______	(say hello)	sample	______	(easy)
pedal	______	(an award)	laughter	______	(female child)
belief	______	(end of worries)	fresh	______	(meat)
project	______	(look after)	carry	______	(Indian spice)

4 Change each word to an adjective by adding **ible** or **able**.

rely	flex	change	adore	respect
______	______	______	______	______
sense	comfort	terror	value	misery
______	______	______	______	______

Spelling Rules! Student Book 3 (ISBN 9780655092605) © Janelle Ho, Helen Pearson

5 Change each word to a noun by adding **ion** or **ment**.

govern	treat	express	direct	complete
________	________	________	________	________
separate	move	argue	explain	attach
________	________	________	________	________

6 Say each word. Circle the stressed syllable and underline the schwa(s).

dollar	quiet	above	territory	freedom
awesome	wrinkle	elephant	experience	disappointment

7 Write the letters that represent the schwa.

____sleep Aug____st fict____n quart____ for____gn

envir____nm____nt mount____n neighb____ choc____l____te

8 Circle the word that does not make sense. Write the correct word.

I helped my little sister carry the two-milligram bag of rice. ____________

Everyone was hungry after a long day's tucker. ____________

I was amused when the baby stuck her tong out at me. ____________

As part of the holiday, we'll go for a river ride in a taboo. ____________

The deer fearfully defended her fawn against the lion. ____________

After Jenna finishes university, she's going to Mr Smith's Year 1 class. ____________

Your taking too long! I'm going to walk behind. ____________ ____________

9 Which tip or rule do you find most useful? How has it helped you?

____

____

____

____

List words in unit order

Unit 1
brave
shade
brake
table
awake
aeroplane
while
beside
spite
alive
advise
promise

Unit 2
close
alone
erode
suppose
approve
wardrobe
huge
pure
cube
refuse
accuse
conclude

Unit 3
shook
blood
choose
soothe
bleed
breath
breathe
threat
explain
throat
poach
cockroach

Unit 4
know
growl
below
allow
touch
grouchy
pounce
mountain
royal
money
trolley
layer

Unit 5
arch
coach
attach
clench
monarch
technology
chemical
scheme
parachute
sketch
scratch
butcher

Unit 7
grief
relief
fierce
niece
sieve
thieve
believe
friend
weird
receive
ceiling
foreign

Unit 8
taut
haul
fault
pause
sauce
sausage
audio
flaw
thaw
drawer
sprawl
awesome

Unit 9
gallop
collide
swallow
channel
tennis
rubbish
common
lesson
borrow
attempt
affect
effect

Unit 10
saddle
waddle
struggle
scribble
settle
drizzle
grumble
candle
stable
wobble
syllable
startle

Unit 11
January
February
March
April
May
June
July
August
September
October
November
December

Unit 13
gather
guest
guide
together
germ
gentle
genius
giant
large
stage
gigantic
gypsy

Unit 14
quiet
quite
queue
quarter
squirm
squeal
squawk
equal
request
require
squirrel
mosquito

Unit 15
delight
midnight
frighten
frightful
neighbour
height
straight
enough
though
through
daughter
naughty

Unit 16
laugh
toughen
graph
photograph
autograph
elephant
telephone
sphere
trophy
alphabet
phrase
physical

Unit 17
puff
cliff
staff
shelf
wolf
scarf
wharf
thief
knife
handkerchief
yourself
giraffe

Unit 19
wrinkle
wrestle
knead
knowledge
gnaw
gnome
hour
honest
island
tongue
doubt
ghost

Unit 20
across
always
about
around
almost
already
ahead
asleep
above

Spelling Rules! Student Book 3 (ISBN 9780655092605) © Janelle Ho, Helen Pearson

another
along
altogether

Unit 21

untidy
unlikely
mischief
misplace
misbehave
mistake
disagree
disgrace
disgusting
dishonest
disobey
discover

Unit 22

country
state
northern
western
south
capital
territory
Australia
New South Wales
Victoria
Tasmania
Queensland

Unit 23

Mob
Elder
Aunty
Uncle
deadly
gammon
tucker
humpy
yakka
yidaki
boomerang
marngrook

Unit 25

harm**ful**
peace**ful**
colour**ful**
grate**ful**
boast**ful**
plenti**ful**
beauti**ful**
help**less**
use**less**
care**less**
fear**less**
life**less**

Unit 26

kind**ness**
happi**ness**
revis**ion**
televis**ion**
direct**ion**
friend**ship**
king**dom**
free**dom**
for**wards**
back**wards**
child**hood**
neighbour**hood**

Unit 27

metre
kilometre
centimetre
millimetre
litre
gram
decade
uniform
bicycle
triangle
dozen
dollar

Unit 28

exit
extra
expert
experience
extreme
example
exact
excuse
excellent
exclaim
excite
exercise

Unit 29

her**o**
pian**o**
zer**o**
radi**o**
t**oe**
can**oe**
kangar**oo**
tab**oo**
sof**a**
dram**a**
ide**a**
er**a**

Unit 31

sta**tion**
fic**tion**
sec**tion**
frac**tion**
cush**ion**
fash**ion**
miss**ion**
express**ion**
relig**ion**
mill**ion**
champ**ion**
informa**tion**

Unit 32

move**ment**
state**ment**
argu**ment**
amaze**ment**
measure**ment**
govern**ment**
environ**ment**
treat**ment**
develop**ment**
attach**ment**
encourage**ment**
disappoint**ment**

Unit 33

reli**able**
cap**able**
ador**able**
avail**able**
comfort**able**
miser**able**
valu**able**
horr**ible**
terr**ible**
sens**ible**
flex**ible**
respons**ible**

Unit 34

igloo
robot
yacht
iceberg
khaki
tsunami
kindergarten
kowtow
pizza
spaghetti
chocolate
restaurant

LIST WORDS IN ALPHABETICAL ORDER

about	Unit 20
above	Unit 20
accuse	Unit 2
across	Unit 20
adorable	Unit 33
advise	Unit 1
aeroplane	Unit 1
affect	Unit 9
ahead	Unit 20
alive	Unit 1
allow	Unit 4
almost	Unit 20
alone	Unit 2
along	Unit 20
alphabet	Unit 16
altogether	Unit 20
already	Unit 20
always	Unit 20
amazement	Unit 32
another	Unit 20
approve	Unit 2
April	Unit 11
arch	Unit 5
argument	Unit 32
around	Unit 20
asleep	Unit 20
attach	Unit 5
attachment	Unit 32
attempt	Unit 9
audio	Unit 8
August	Unit 11
Aunty	Unit 23
Australia	Unit 22
autograph	Unit 16
awake	Unit 1
awesome	Unit 8
backwards	Unit 26
beautiful	Unit 25
believe	Unit 7
below	Unit 4
bicycle	Unit 27
bleed	Unit 3
blood	Unit 3
boastful	Unit 25
boomerang	Unit 23
borrow	Unit 9
brake	Unit 1
brave	Unit 1
breath	Unit 3
breathe	Unit 3
butcher	Unit 5
candle	Unit 10
canoe	Unit 29
capable	Unit 33
capital	Unit 22
careless	Unit 25
ceiling	Unit 7
centimetre	Unit 27
champion	Unit 31
channel	Unit 9
chemical	Unit 5
childhood	Unit 26
chocolate	Unit 34
choose	Unit 3
clench	Unit 5
cliff	Unit 17
close	Unit 2
coach	Unit 5
cockroach	Unit 3
collide	Unit 9
colourful	Unit 25
comfortable	Unit 33
common	Unit 9
conclude	Unit 2
confuse	Unit 2
country	Unit 22
cube	Unit 2
cushion	Unit 31
daughter	Unit 15
deadly	Unit 23
decade	Unit 27
December	Unit 11
delight	Unit 15
development	Unit 32
direction	Unit 26
disagree	Unit 21
disappointment	Unit 32
discover	Unit 21
disgrace	Unit 21
disgusting	Unit 21
dishonest	Unit 21
disobey	Unit 21
dollar	Unit 27
doubt	Unit 19
dozen	Unit 27
drama	Unit 29
drawer	Unit 8
drizzle	Unit 10
echo	Unit 29
effect	Unit 9
Elder	Unit 23
encouragement	Unit 32
enough	Unit 15
environment	Unit 32
elephant	Unit 16
equal	Unit 14
era	Unit 29
exact	Unit 28
example	Unit 28
excellent	Unit 28
excite	Unit 28
exclaim	Unit 28
excuse	Unit 28
exercise	Unit 28
exit	Unit 28
experience	Unit 28
expert	Unit 28
explain	Unit 3
expression	Unit 31
extra	Unit 28
extreme	Unit 28
fashion	Unit 31
fault	Unit 8
fearless	Unit 25
February	Unit 11
fiction	Unit 31
fierce	Unit 7
flaw	Unit 8
flexible	Unit 33
foreign	Unit 7
forwards	Unit 26
fraction	Unit 31
freedom	Unit 26
friend	Unit 7
friendship	Unit 26
frighten	Unit 15
frightful	Unit 15
gammon	Unit 23
gallop	Unit 9
gather	Unit 13
genius	Unit 13
gentle	Unit 13
germ	Unit 13
ghost	Unit 19
giant	Unit 13
gigantic	Unit 13
giraffe	Unit 17
gnaw	Unit 19
gnome	Unit 19
government	Unit 32
gram	Unit 27
graph	Unit 16
grateful	Unit 25
grief	Unit 7
grouchy	Unit 4
growl	Unit 4
grumble	Unit 10
guest	Unit 13
guide	Unit 13
gypsy	Unit 13
handkerchief	Unit 17
happiness	Unit 26
harmful	Unit 25
haul	Unit 8
height	Unit 15
helpless	Unit 25
hero	Unit 29
honest	Unit 19
horrible	Unit 33
hour	Unit 19
huge	Unit 2
humpy	Unit 23
iceberg	Unit 34
idea	Unit 29
igloo	Unit 34
information	Unit 31
island	Unit 19

January	Unit 11
July	Unit 11
June	Unit 11
kangaroo	Unit 29
khaki	Unit 34
kilometre	Unit 27
kindergarten	Unit 34
kindness	Unit 26
kingdom	Unit 26
knead	Unit 19
knife	Unit 17
know	Unit 4
knowledge	Unit 19
kowtow	Unit 34
large	Unit 13
laugh	Unit 16
layer	Unit 4
lesson	Unit 9
lifeless	Unit 25
litre	Unit 27
March	Unit 11
marngrook	Unit 23
May	Unit 11
measurement	Unit 32
metre	Unit 27
midnight	Unit 15
millimetre	Unit 27
million	Unit 31
misbehave	Unit 21
mischief	Unit 21
miserable	Unit 33
misplace	Unit 21
mission	Unit 31
mistake	Unit 21
Mob	Unit 23
monarch	Unit 5
money	Unit 4
mosquito	Unit 14
mountain	Unit 4
movement	Unit 32
naughty	Unit 15
neighbour	Unit 15
neighbourhood	Unit 26
New South Wales	Unit 22
niece	Unit 7
northern	Unit 22
November	Unit 11
October	Unit 11
parachute	Unit 5
pause	Unit 8
peaceful	Unit 25
photograph	Unit 16
phrase	Unit 16
physical	Unit 16
piano	Unit 29
pizza	Unit 34
plentiful	Unit 25
poach	Unit 3
pounce	Unit 4
promise	Unit 1
puff	Unit 17
pure	Unit 2
quarter	Unit 14
Queensland	Unit 22
queue	Unit 14
quiet	Unit 14
quite	Unit 14
radio	Unit 29
receive	Unit 7
refuse	Unit 2
reliable	Unit 33
relief	Unit 7
religion	Unit 31
request	Unit 14
require	Unit 14
responsible	Unit 33
restaurant	Unit 34
revision	Unit 26
robot	Unit 34
royal	Unit 4
rubbish	Unit 9
saddle	Unit 10
sauce	Unit 8
sausage	Unit 8
scarf	Unit 17
scheme	Unit 5
scratch	Unit 5
scribble	Unit 10
section	Unit 31
sensible	Unit 33
September	Unit 11
settle	Unit 10
shade	Unit 1
shelf	Unit 17
shook	Unit 3
sieve	Unit 7
sketch	Unit 5
sofa	Unit 29
soothe	Unit 3
south	Unit 22
spaghetti	Unit 34
sphere	Unit 16
spite	Unit 1
sprawl	Unit 8
squawk	Unit 14
squeal	Unit 14
squirm	Unit 14
squirrel	Unit 14
stable	Unit 10
staff	Unit 17
stage	Unit 13
startle	Unit 10
state	Unit 22
statement	Unit 32
station	Unit 31
straight	Unit 15
struggle	Unit 10
suppose	Unit 2
swallow	Unit 9
syllable	Unit 10
table	Unit 1
taboo	Unit 29
Tasmania	Unit 22
taut	Unit 8
technology	Unit 5
telephone	Unit 16
television	Unit 26
tennis	Unit 9
terrible	Unit 33
territory	Unit 22
thaw	Unit 8
thief	Unit 17
thieve	Unit 7
though	Unit 15
threat	Unit 3
throat	Unit 3
through	Unit 15
toe	Unit 29
together	Unit 13
tongue	Unit 19
touch	Unit 4
toughen	Unit 16
treatment	Unit 32
triangle	Unit 27
trolley	Unit 4
trophy	Unit 16
tsunami	Unit 34
tucker	Unit 23
Uncle	Unit 23
uniform	Unit 27
unlikely	Unit 21
untidy	Unit 21
useless	Unit 25
valuable	Unit 33
Victoria	Unit 22
waddle	Unit 10
wardrobe	Unit 2
weird	Unit 7
western	Unit 22
wharf	Unit 17
while	Unit 1
white	Unit 1
wobble	Unit 10
wolf	Unit 17
wrestle	Unit 19
wrinkle	Unit 19
yacht	Unit 34
yakka	Unit 23
yidaki	Unit 23
yourself	Unit 17

SPELLING RULES AND TIPS

To make a plural

If a noun ends in **o**, the plural usually ends in **es**.

echo → *echoes*

If the word ends in two vowels, just add **s**.

kangaroo → *kangaroos* *radio* → *radios*

If a noun ends in **f** or **fe**, change the **f** or **fe** to **v** and add **es** to form the plural.

elf → *elves* *life* → *lives*

If a noun ends in **ff** or **ffe**, add **s** to form the plural.

cliff → *cliffs* *giraffe* → *giraffes*

Past tense

Most verbs show the past tense by adding **ed**.

discover → *discovered*

Some verbs have a different form in the past tense.

write → *wrote*

Adding ful and ness

If a word ends with a short **y**, change **y** to **i** before adding **ful**.

beauty → *beautiful*

If an adjective ends with a short **y**, change **y** to **i** before adding **ness**.

happy → *happiness*

When you add a **prefix**, do not remove any letters. If the prefix ends in the same letter the base word starts with, keep both letters.

un + noticed → *unnoticed*

dis + similar → *dissimilar*

When **c** is followed by **e**, **i** or **y**, it usually sounds like **s**.
When **g** is followed by **e**, **i** or **y**, it usually sounds like **j**.

Synonyms are words with similar meanings.

Small and *little* are synonyms.

Antonyms are words with the opposite meaning.

Full and *empty* are antonyms.

Antonyms can be formed using prefixes or suffixes.

kind ***un**kind* *harm**ful*** *harm**less***

Use an **apostrophe** to show that someone owns something.

Tim's bag